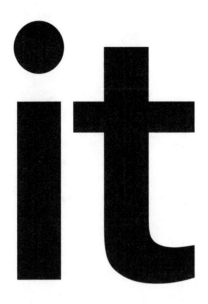

CRAIG GROESCHEL

ZONDERVAN.com/
AUTHORTRACKER
follow your favorite authors

ZONDERVAN

It
Copyright © 2008 by Craig Groeschel

This title is also available as a Zondervan ebook.
Visit www.zondervan.com/ebooks.

This title is also available in a Zondervan audio edition.
Visit www.zondervan.fm.

Requests for information should be addressed to:
Zondervan, *Grand Rapids, Michigan* 49530

Library of Congress Cataloging-in-Publication Data

Groeschel, Craig.
   It : how churches and leaders can get it and keep it / Craig Groeschel.
        p. cm.
     Includes bibliographical references.
     ISBN 978-0-310-28682-0 (hardcover)
     1. Church. 2. Church renewal. 3. Religious awakening — Christianity. I. Title.
   BV600.3.G75 2008
   269 — dc22   2008009578

Interior design by Mark Sheeres

Cover design by Rob Monacelli

Printed in the United States of America

10 11 12 13 14 15 16 • 25 24 23 22 21 20 19 18 17 16 15 14 13 12 11 10

For my friends and family
at LifeChurch.tv
I love you all and thank God for you.
You have *it*!

CONTENTS

PART 1 • WHAT IS it?

PART 2 • WHAT CONTRIBUTES TO it?

PART 3 • WHAT IT MEANS TO GET it BACK AND GUARD it

LIST OF PROFILES

ACKNOWLEDGMENTS

To all of my friends who offered me support, encouragement, and assistance, I'm very grateful.

I am especially indebted to:

Paul Engle, Brian Phipps, Mike Cook, and the whole team at Zondervan: it is an honor to partner with you.

Vince Antonucci and Brian Smith: your contribution was amazing. Thank you for your help and friendship.

Anna Meadows, Abbi Zeliff, John Davis, Allyson Evans, Brannon Golden: thank you so much for reading through the rough draft. Your feedback and suggestions made a huge difference.

Bobby Gruenewald, Jerry Hurley, Kevin Penry, Sam Roberts: I appreciate your help and thoughts on *It*. More so, I'm grateful for your integrity and leadership at the church. You are great friends. See you at the fire pit.

Aaron Ball, Sarah McLean, and Lance Young: thanks for helping to find the right pictures for *It*. I'm honored to serve Jesus with you.

Catie, Mandy, Anna, Sam, Bookie, and Jo: I love you so much I could pop!

Amy: you are my dream girl on steroids!

YOU KNOW it WHEN YOU SEE it

It.

Some ministries have *it*. Some don't.

Most churches want *it*. Few have *it*.

When a church has *it*, everyone can tell. And when one doesn't … everyone can tell.

The same is true with leaders. Some leaders have *it*. Some don't. And *it* or *it*-lessness is obvious.

It is always unique. *It* is always powerful. *It* is always life-changing.

That's *its* upside. *It* has another side too. *It* attracts critics. *It* is controversial. Many people misunderstand *it*. *It*'s hard to find, but *it*'s impossible to miss.

By now you're probably asking, *What is it?* My answer is …

I don't know.

Really, I don't.

Here's what I do know: if you've ever been part of a ministry that had *it*, you knew you were part of something special. In other words, you knew *it* when you saw *it*. And *it* was an awesome work of God that couldn't be contained, couldn't be harnessed, and couldn't be explained.

If you've never seen *it* up close, ask around and see if you can find *it*. Just listen to what people in your community are saying. I promise, if *it* has come to a ministry near you, people are talking about *it*. When a ministry has *it*, the ground seems to rumble. Everyone hears about *it*. "You *have* to visit this church. What's going on there is incredible. Trust me. You have to check *it* out."

And people do check out an *it*-filled church. Not only do they kick the tires but many of them actually join *it*. They seem to intuitively grasp whatever *it* is. To an outsider with a critical heart, these converts simply drank the Kool-Aid and became fanatics. But to those who experience *it*, life is different. They're changed. They're passionate. They're excited. They know they're part of what God's doing. And they want everyone to know about *it*.

If you're still not sure what I'm talking about, this book should shed some light on *it* for you. You might be thinking, *But I don't understand* it. *Aren't some people just born with* it *while others never find* it? Without a doubt, *it* is a gift from God, who is *its* only source. But I believe that God makes *it* available to anyone who wants *it*. I believe he wants to give *it* to you and your ministry. That may be difficult for you to believe, but it's true.

While I certainly can't promise *it* to you, I can encourage you toward *it*. Together we'll discover a few simple principles that could ignite *it* in your heart, life, and ministry. I'll be praying that the ministry you love will find *it*.

And never lose *it*.

PART ONE

WHAT IS it?

> The wind blows
> wherever it pleases.
> You hear its sound,
> but you cannot tell
> where it comes from
> or where it is going.
> So it is with everyone
> born of the Spirit.
>
> —*Jesus (John 3:8)*

A few things that cannot be observed directly but can be detected only indirectly:

Love

Gravity

God the Father

Black holes

Freedom

God the Holy Spirit

Magnetism

Truth

Infinity

It

ONE

WHERE DID it COME FROM?

You either have it or you don't.

—*Popular saying*

for years, I've been intrigued by *it*. In 1991, I became an associate pastor of a church that was starting to get *it*. During my five years with this church, God truly gave *it* to us. The church doubled in size. We baptized hundreds of people. God was glorified.

The church continued to enjoy *it* for close to a decade. One day, though no one noticed at first, *it* started to fade. Although still a strong ministry, this church doesn't have *it* like they used to. What once was dead, then alive, is dead again. After watching the church being blessed with *it*, many people mourn that that same church is now, years later, futilely fighting for life without *it*.

You could say *it* happens.

But not always.

In 1996, my wife, Amy, and I started a new church that's now called LifeChurch.tv. In those early years, we didn't have anything most churches have (and think are necessary). In fact, everything we had was junk. We met in a borrowed two-car garage that smelled just like … a garage. On the first weekend of our new church, we experienced a rare Oklahoma snowstorm. I still remember the people huddling together to stay warm, wearing their winter hats and gloves for the entire service.

Since I knew the importance of caring for children, we reserved the best facilities for those under five years of age. Our children met for children's church in a large storage closet. (This gave a whole new meaning, at the end of each service, to the phrase "coming out of the closet.") We had one temperamental microphone and two borrowed speakers. We borrowed seventy-five green, felt-backed chairs from hell. (All felt-backed chairs are from hell and should be returned there as soon as possible.) The garage was so dark we bought a floodlight from the hardware store for $19.99 to light it. This innovation worked great until one day the light exploded during a sermon. People thought terrorists were attacking and dove for cover. On a positive note, several people accepted Christ that day. (And Edna Mae's counselors at the psychiatric hospital tell us she's doing much better.)

Today, LifeChurch.tv has a reputation for using technology whenever possible. In the early days, we were excited if something we plugged in didn't blow up, including our hand-me-down early-1970s overhead projector.

For those of you who don't know what an overhead projector is, I'll explain. An overhead projector was *the* state-of-the-art, cutting-edge way (in 1976; unfortunately this was 1996) to display song lyrics on a screen. Or in our case, on the garage door. This ministry-changing innovation fell on the technology scale somewhere between printed hymnals in the pews in Guten-

WHAT IS it?

berg's day and today's triple video projectors casting shimmering images onto oversized screens. (Ah, the good old days.)

To use the overhead projector — commonly referred to simply as the "overhead" (because that's part of its name but also because the advanced lightbulb-and-lens technology was so mysterious that it went right over the heads of all of us laypersons) — you'd type the words on a sheet of transparent plastic, place it on the bed of the projector, and *voila*! Worship magic. Our skilled transparency flipper was Jerome, who had lost a finger to a gunshot wound in a drug deal gone bad. (Yes, the drug thing was *before* he became a Christian. But he was still a new believer, and for a hundred dollars he would have made anyone disappear for me.) New people were mesmerized by the light shining onto the garage door, following it to its source and then silently counting Jerome's fingers: *One, two, three, four ... Four?*

Exquisite Intensity

Why am I telling you all of this? Well, it's cheaper than counseling. But I also want you to understand: we didn't have anything that most people think you need to have church.

We didn't have a nice building. We didn't have our own office. We didn't have a church phone number (unless you count my home phone number). We didn't have a paid staff. We didn't have a logo. We didn't have a website. We didn't serve Starbucks. We didn't have sermon series with clever titles lifted from *Baywatch* episodes.

What *did* we have? We had a few people; you could count them on both hands. (Well, Jerome couldn't, but *you* could.) Those few people were off-the-charts excited about Jesus. We had enough Bibles to go around. And we had *it*.

At the time, I didn't call it *it*. But we were definitely full of *it*. (Which is ironic, because I've been accused many times of being full of it.) Even though we didn't know what *it* was, we knew *it* was from God. And *it* was special.

Whatever *it* was, everyone who came felt *it*. And they talked about it. And new people came and experienced *it*. And the church grew. And grew. And lives were changed by the dozens. Then by the hundreds. Then by the thousands.

Ten years later, we were thrilled to be ministering to thousands of people at thirteen different locations in six states. As exciting as that sounds (and it was), after a while I started to notice something that made me pause. Over time, it made me nervous. Finally, it started to bother me deeply.

In some locations, we were losing *it*.

Even though I had never known what caused *it*, I had always hoped we'd never lose *it*. And yet we were. Although some campuses unquestionably still had *it*, in other locations, we had to admit that *it* seemed to have quit. That distinct spiritual hum, so obvious before, was harder to hear. The life-changing stories that were once a part of every discussion were fewer and farther between.

Instead of passionately caring about people who didn't have Christ, members started to gripe about how the church wasn't all that they wanted it to be. Instead of people sacrificing for the cause of Christ, people appeared to be consuming, not contributing.

Where did *it* go?

Did we kill *it*?

Did God take *it* away?

Random *it*-ness?

In the past, I figured that if a church didn't have *it*, it was, at least to some extent, the leadership's fault. The elders must not have been focused or passionate or praying or *something*. Or the senior pastor hadn't cast a compelling Christ-focused vision, or he didn't preach hard enough or wasn't inspiring people to become like Christ. Or the staff had gotten tired, bored, or lazy.

Surely someone was to blame.

Suddenly, I had a problem. All of our campuses were under the same leadership. The buildings were similar. The worship pastors were unique but had consistent styles. The kids' curriculum never varied from campus to campus. All were experiencing exactly the same weekend teaching. But some campuses had *it*. And some didn't.

Think about this. All of our buildings intentionally have a similar look and feel. We work hard to cultivate exactly the same values, culture, and leadership on every campus. We hire all staff members through the same process. Each weekend, the people attending in one location hear the same message as the people at every other location. Sure, some of our campus pastors are better leaders than others. And ministering in different cities and states will certainly produce different results. Yet our *it*-ness apparently was randomly distributed from site to site.

Some campuses had huge numbers of conversions, while others struggled to lead anyone to Christ. Those with many coming to Christ had more than enough volunteers. The others were struggling to fill a quota. At the with-*it* campuses, giving was growing. The *it*-less were financially stagnant. One campus tripled in size in one year, while growth in others was flat. Two grew to more than two thousand people in a year. That same year, one shrank.

Guess which one got smaller? The one where *I* taught ... live and in person. All the campuses that experienced weekly video teaching grew. (If you don't like video teaching, put *that* in your pipe and smoke it.)

As I dug deeper, I realized that not only did the *campuses* have varying degress of *it*-fulness but *individual teams* did too. In the same location, one team might have *it*, while another might not.

Thinking about other churches and ministries, I realized I could name a dozen that used to have *it* but don't anymore. At one time, they were reaching tons of people, growing with cutting-edge ministry innovations. But somewhere along the journey, they seemed to freeze in time, then slowly thaw and melt away. They had once had *it*. But they lost *it*.

Could that be happening to us?

Then I watched a few other churches whose growth had been flat for years. One day, something changed. Maybe they got a new leader. Or their previous leader found a second wind. Perhaps God gave a staff member an idea that worked. I don't know, it could be that they redecorated the church in God's favorite color. Whatever the reason, I could think of many churches that didn't have *it* for years but got *it*. Sudden, dramatic resuscitation.

Two important principles, or *It* Factors, dawned on me:

- The good news: if you don't have *it*, you can get *it*.
- The bad news: if you have *it*, you can lose *it*.

Questions for Discussion or Reflection

1 If a church lacks what most people think you need to have church, yet they have *it*, does this mean that buildings, environments, logos, websites, and so on are not important? Why or why not?

2 Can you think of an example of a church that had *it* and then lost it? Describe what happened. Why do you think that ministry lost *it*?

3 If you've ever been part of a ministry that had *it*, you knew it. Describe what *it* felt like. What were some of the qualities that you experienced and appreciated?

4 What part of your ministry has *it*? (Your choir, student ministry, or hospitality ministry might have *it*.) What factors do you believe contribute to *it*?

WHAT IS *it*?

TWO

SOME HAVE it, SOME LACK it

> The perfect church service would be one we were almost unaware of. Our attention would have been on God.
>
> —*C. S. Lewis*

When I was a sophomore in college, I became a Christ-follower. I had been a beer-drinking, skirt-chasing, hell-raising frat boy. Suddenly I was a Jesus freak. Even as a brand-new believer, somehow I knew I needed to find a church.

From the little experience and knowledge I had of church, I believed churches were all pretty much the same. So I didn't have a well-defined set of criteria for what I was looking for in a church; I simply went searching for the coolest looking one. Finally I found it, a gorgeous, genuine historical church.

This church had *everything*: stained-glass windows, a mile-high steeple, and best of all, a huge bell. (I had no idea why it needed a bell, but still I was impressed. Even to this day I suffer from a bit of bell envy.)

The only thing this church lacked was *it*. In fact, if there's an opposite of *it*, a kind of anti-*it*, null-*it*, zilch-*it*, nada-*it*, zip-*it*, that's what they had. But I didn't realize this until later.

I did my best to make a good first impression at my new church home. I didn't own a suit, so I wore my best khakis, my braided leather belt, shiny penny loafers, and a wrinkly white shirt (no tie), with my hair perfectly parted down the middle and feathered on the sides. (Give me a break. It was the eighties.) I looked like I had walked straight off the set of *Miami Vice*, except, of course, I was wearing socks. (And didn't live in a houseboat with an alligator named Elvis, though that was part of my ten-year plan.)

I remember climbing up the front stairs for about half a mile, headed for the massive, perfectly carved wooden doors. (I won't even tell you about my door envy.) The usher (or greeter or bouncer, whatever church people call that guy) looked like he'd just eaten a nice bowl of horseradish. He glared at me and offered this delightful welcome: "Son, we dress up for God here." Since I was a new believer with an unrenewed mind, I thought something like, *How'd you like to meet God face-to-face right now?! You sorry little . . .*

My next greeting was inside, where a disdainful usher looked me up and down, gauging whether he should waste one of his bulletins on me. Evidently, I was bulletin worthy. But just barely.

Clutching my new treasure, I walked reverently into the beautiful, mostly empty sanctuary. Since I didn't want to be tardy my first time, I had arrived several minutes before the service was scheduled to start. I assumed the crowd wouldn't show up until precisely on time. A few people mingled, but no one said hello to me . . . or to anyone else they didn't know. A couple of people were already seated, scattered around here and there, alone. I took my cue from them and found a seat. A minute later, a white-haired woman with a vinegary scowl scolded me for sitting in her seat. I wondered to myself whether a section of a wooden bench could even be called a seat, whether she had first claimed this "seat" in 1879, and why she couldn't just sit her grouchy butt in one of the four vacant rows nearby. But instead of claiming squatter's rights, I muttered something about not getting her Depends undergarments in a bunch, got up, and found a new place to sit. It wasn't hard. The place was nearly empty.

And the crowd never showed.

Finally a man in a gown sauntered regally to the podium and with arms outstretched offered in a very pastoral voice, "Greetings in the name of the Lord." Everyone mumbled something that I couldn't understand, stood up almost as one, and the organ sputtered to life. We sang three hymns like we were lifeless robots. It was comforting, I guess, but odd. The passionate words in these ancient songs were some of the most beautiful I'd ever read — at least the words I recognized.

For each hymn, we sang verses one, two ... and four. What did they have against verse three? Or perhaps someone had abducted all of the verse threes? (Had they notified the proper authorities?) I've been a believer for twenty years now. To this day, I've never heard a satisfactory answer to that question.

After the songs, another guy in a gown came up, less regally, and droned some announcements. Finally, we came to the feature presentation. The guy with the nicest, fanciest gown — I assumed he was the big pastor — got up to deliver a sermon that would feed our hungry souls. He talked. And he talked and he talked. And I stayed hungry.

When he finally finished, everyone got up and left unceremoniously. I dutifully followed the flow of traffic out the door and got in my car. On my drive home, I was bewildered, struggling to understand why God — this God who had so radically flipped my life upside down, who breathed into me a new life and new passion — would demand that I waste my Sunday mornings like this.

As I said earlier, I had no idea what *it* was, but I could feel *its* absence. And, I figured, if *that* beautiful, majestic church didn't have *it*, what hope did I have of finding *it* in any other church?

Cathedral of the Devoted Dead

As I reflect on that experience now, I can still remember it vividly. No one was friendly (at least not to an outsider). No one smiled. Only a few people sang. No one told me they were glad I came. No one seemed excited about anything. Even when the service was over, no one invited me back. It was as if the church had died years before, but no one had noticed.

I returned to my college campus disappointed and a little confused. It was lunchtime, so I went to the cafeteria for some food, or at least our cafeteria's version of food. I was distracted from my wannabe corn dog by a boisterous group of about twenty students who came in laughing, cutting up, talking over each other. And carrying Bibles.

They had my attention. I watched them carefully, trying not to look like I was staring at them. They prayed before they ate. But they didn't just "say grace." They *prayed*. With sincerity. For an uncomfortably long time.

As they began eating, their relational electricity resumed. When I couldn't stand it anymore, I got up and walked in their direction. As I approached, one guy's head whipped around toward me, and a broad smile spread across his face. He sprang up and lunged toward me with his hand extended. "Is it true? Is it true? We heard ..." He trailed off. "Did you *really* find Christ?"

He and I bonded instantly. His eyes welled up with tears as he told me that he and others had been praying for me to come to Christ for over a year. I was stunned. Speechless. Humbled. Blown away. And overwhelmed with gratitude. *Someone has been praying? For me? How did they know? I've been hurting so badly. I've been so far from God, so desperate. Searching for something, anything. How did they know?*

He invited me to join them and introduced me to everyone at the table. These people were different. Passionate, godly, sincere, authentic, transparent, hungry for Christ. *It* was instantly recognizable, too obvious to miss.

After just a few minutes talking together, they invited me to come to church with them — that same night. Like me, most of them had just come from church. How could someone possibly *want* to go to church twice in one day?

And yet, they wanted to go. I found out later, the reason was that their church had *it*.

They insisted that I dress casually, so when I met them later, I was wearing my O.P. shorts and my favorite blue T-shirt. Clutching my shiny, green, crisp, pocket-sized Gideon New Testament, I hopped into the car with several others. As we approached their church, I was confused again. It just didn't make any sense. The building didn't look anything like a church. It wasn't pretty at all. It was just a plain metal structure. Actually, calling it plain is being generous. It wasn't even decent. It was ugly. Like "U-G-L-Y, you ain't got no alibi" ugly.

Since traffic was backed up for half a block, we had to wait a long time, but no one seemed to mind or even notice. Old people, young people, rich people, poor people, every kind of person you can imagine was making their way inside. There were whites, African-Americans, Asians, Latinos. All kinds of people. When we finally parked the car and headed in, I was swarmed by smiling people welcoming me. Several people warmly greeted me as I entered the building. One guy even gave me a hug.

Inside, nothing about this building was special. And even if there had been something worth noticing, I would have missed it because of all the people.

They ... were ... everywhere.

And it was loud. It was like a happening nightclub with a party atmosphere. And that was just the lobby. But instead of immorality, smoking, and alcohol, I found warm smiles, loving hugs, and Bibles everywhere. The room was electric. The fire marshal probably would have had a stroke if he had seen it.

Riding the *It* Wave

Something special was about to happen. Everyone there knew it. They weren't just anticipating *it*; they were positively *expecting it*. Of course, I had no idea what to expect when I agreed to come, but now I was expecting *it* too. Even I knew something was going to happen.

We were still in the lobby when music started to come through a double doorway. Like a hungry amoeba, this swarm of people rushed in. We rode the wave into ... What would you call a big room like that? A sanctuary? An auditorium? A multipurpose room? A great place for a killer game of dodgeball?

With its contagiously exciting atmosphere, it didn't really matter what you called it.

People there loved God, and they were ecstatic to have the opportunity to express their hearts. Some cried. Some lifted their hands. (*What's that about?* I wondered.) Some knelt in prayer.

When the preacher walked up to speak, he had something about him that's hard to describe. He seemed confident, but it was so much more than that. He looked confident and humble at the same time. He was *glowing*. It was as if he'd just gotten off the phone with God, and God had given him a message to share with us. He smiled knowingly.

As the preacher began to speak, people leaned in, listening intently, as if every word mattered. His words pierced my heart, as though he were speaking directly to me. To this day, more than twenty years later, I remember certain details of that message. His message impacted me. The church impacted me. The people impacted me. Through it all, God impacted me.

When I met Christ, I became a different person. Forgiven. Changed. And new. Experiencing God at the church was similar to my moment of salvation. It was like another turning point. Somehow I experienced God in a new and deeper way. My desire for him wasn't about what he could do for me. It was just a desire for him and nothing else. From that day forward I was somehow a different kind of person. God was no longer just someone who did something for me. I was overwhelmed with an awareness that *it* is about me loving him. *It* is about his will. His plan. His desire to reach other people ... through me.

This church had me at "hello." They had *it*. I wanted *it*. I needed *it*.

And I got *it*.

- Beautiful buildings, cool environments, and the right technology aren't necessary to have *it*.
- A person surrendered fully to Christ gets *it*. And once a person has *it*, he can't keep *it* to himself.

it FACTORS

Questions for Discussion or Reflection

1 Have you ever visited a church that had everything and yet didn't have *it*? What happened? How did you feel? What can you learn from these experiences?

2 Think about some people you know who have *it*. Describe what it is about them that is contagious.

3 Sometimes when another local ministry has *it*, a natural response to not understanding *it* is to become critical of *it*. What local ministry do you know of that has *it*? What do you think they do that contributes to *it*? What do you think you could learn from them?

4 Every ministry has strengths and weaknesses. How does your ministry excel? What part of your ministry is best helping people get *it*? What part of your ministry needs to be developed to better help people experience *it*?

THREE

BRINGING **it** INTO FOCUS

I shall not today attempt further to define the kinds of material I understand to be embraced within that shorthand description [pornography]; and perhaps I could never succeed in intelligibly doing so. But *I know it when I see it*, and the motion picture involved in this case is not that.

—Supreme Court Justice Potter Stewart

i can't tell you exactly what *it* is. Part of what makes it *it* is that *it* defies categorization. *It* won't reduce to a memorable slogan. *It* is far more special than that.

That's why we have to embrace the fact that God makes *it* happen. *It* is from him. *It* is by him. *It* is for his glory. We can't create *it*. We can't reproduce *it*. We can't manufacture *it*.

It is not a model. *It* is not a system. *It* is not the result of a program. You can't purchase or manufacture *it*. *It* can't be copied.

Not everyone will get *it*. *It* can't be learned in a classroom. Yet even though *it* can't be taught, *it* can be caught.

Good News about *It*

Here's some good news about *it*: You can find *it* in all types of churches. *It* is in traditional churches, charismatic churches, seeker-sensitive churches, purpose-driven churches, emergent churches, and submergent churches. (Okay, I made up that last category.) You can find it in nondenominational churches, Assembly of God churches, Evangelical Covenant churches, Baptist churches, Bible churches, Lutheran churches, Methodist churches, and Episcopalian churches.

Even though you can find *it* in all of these places, you can also go to thousands of these same types of churches that *don't* have *it*.

But whenever God gives *it* to you, *it* is unmistakable.

Based on my experience as a pastor and leadership consultant, here are some observations I can offer you about *it*.

It Works

When a ministry has *it*, most things the leaders try seem to work. If they send out an invitational mailer, new people come — and stick. If they start a singles ministry, it succeeds and grows. If they dream of a mission trip to China, the trip fills, or overfills, and changes the lives of everyone involved. Even when one of their ideas doesn't quite work as planned, just the attempt seems to lead to something new and successful.

For example, for years I was consistently unsuccessful communicating with church members. We tried ten minutes' worth of weekend announcements and put everyone to sleep. We tried the newsletter approach and basically just killed a lot of innocent trees. We attempted e-letters that no one read. Finally after failing our way into a communication-deprived corner, I shot a video to share my heart. I expressed my frustrations, shared my hopes, and requested specific prayers for my family. Then we emailed the video link to the whole membership. The response was off-the-charts amazing. We failed our way to effective communication success.

On the other hand, when a ministry is out of *it*, most of what they try doesn't work. Few new people, if any, show up after the mailer. And those who do often don't return. Their new singles ministry putts along for six months, then *kaput*. And if they

LIFECHURCH.TV

▶   0:00:21 🔊 ▬▬▬▬●

attempt a mission trip to China, they have to cancel it for lack of interest.

When a church has *it*, creativity flows. Everyone comes up with ideas. When a ministry doesn't have *it*, they simply follow the same formula they used the year before. People are bored, uninspired, and complacent.

When a ministry has *it*, the staff knows they're part of something much bigger than themselves, part of a divine mission. They show up early for everything. They often stay late. They rarely fight. When they do disagree, they grow through their differences, usually quickly. When a church doesn't have *it*, the staff is simply doing a job, drawing a paycheck. They're territorial. Jealous. Griping. Even bitter.

Everyone Knows *It*

When a church has *it*, lives are changing, and everyone around knows it. The only thing constant is change, which *it*-soaked people seem to thrive on. When a church doesn't have *it*, few people even notice that no one new is showing up. When someone new does come to church, but looks different, the *it*-free church unintentionally — or sometimes even intentionally — guards the status quo, resisting change.

When a ministry has *it*, everyone can usually feel *it*, but they have trouble describing *it*. Everyone recognizes *it*, but no one knows precisely what *it* is.

Just like with the first church in the New Testament. There, *it* was from God, by God, and for God. Think about the astounding works of God recorded in Acts. No man could have created all that *it*.

Peter — the failure — preached, and three thousand were saved, baptized, and filled with the Spirit of God (Acts 2:41). When the church was persecuted and believers were tortured and often killed, the church, instead of shrinking, grew. If a person had a need, someone else sold their own possessions to meet that need. If someone was arrested for promoting Christ, they would just worship God in prison or lead the jailer to Christ. Occasionally, God would even break them out of jail. One time, a sermon went long, and one drowsy kid drifted off, fell from a second-story window, and was pronounced dead. The disciples raised him back to life. That's some pretty cool *it*.

The first church had *it*! They didn't create *it*. God did. But they did work with *it*. And they made sure not to get in *its* way.

Easy to Misinterpret

So with all this talk about *it*, let's try to put some skin on this concept. It's difficult to define precisely what *it* is, but it's fairly obvious what *it* is not.

Don't miss this, because many people often misinterpret *it*. Someone might visit a growing church and observe outward signs of success — videos, buildings, fancy kids' rooms, and so on. These well-meaning guests mistakenly think, *If we had all that stuff, we'd have* it *too.*

They couldn't be more wrong.

The first-century church in Jerusalem clearly had *it*. And they didn't have any of these fancy accoutrements.

Fast-forward two thousand years. Is *it* still the same? (Yes.) Is *it* still available to us now? (Absolutely!)

So *it* can't possibly be stained-glass windows, hand-carved cherubs, custom silk tapestries, gold-inlaid hymnals, thousand-pipe organs, marble floors, mile-high steeples, hand-painted ceilings, mahogany pews, giant cast-iron bells, and a three-piece, thousand-dollar suit. *It* doesn't stick any better to a young, hip, shaved-headed pastor with rimmed glasses, a goatee, and tattoos than it does to an older, stately gentleman in a robe. Nor is *it* spotlights and lasers, video production, satellite dishes, fog machines, shiny gauze backdrops, four-color glossy brochures, sexy billboards, loud "contemporary" music, free donuts, coffee shops, hip bookstores, break dancing or acrobatics, sermon series named after television shows, a retro-modern matching chair and table onstage, or blue jeans and Heelys. *It* is *not* being on television, being on the internet, or being on book and magazine covers.

It doesn't follow a particular model. You can't copy *it*. You can't ignite *it* within your ministry—or within yourself—just by reading a book. (Not even this one!) (But sorry, no refunds.) Perhaps with a comprehensive list, some careful planning, and enough time and resources you could try to fake *it*. But people would be able to tell.

It is real. *It* is genuine.

Like it or not, *it* is not the result of external factors.

The Best Explanation I Can Give

"So," you may ask, "what is *it*?"

The best explanation I can give you is this: *it* is what God does through a rare combination of these qualities found in his people:

- Passion for his presence
- A deep craving to reach the lost
- Sincere integrity
- Spirit-filled faith
- Down-to-earth humility
- Brokenness

You might ask, "Doesn't God give *it* most often to super-charismatic speakers or turbocharged spiritual leaders? Doesn't *it* show up most around ten-talents people?" Certainly those kinds of leaders can draw a crowd. They can have ministries with an *it*-like appearance. But don't be fooled by imitations. Occasionally you'll see a ministry that apparently has *it*, but in reality, the leader is leading a double life. If *it* is built on sand, *it* is not really *it* and *it* won't last. Without these Christlike qualities, no matter how good things look today, no ministry or leader can sustain *it* with their own talent.

Unfortunately, I can't teach you those qualities. And you can't teach them to me. I wish someone (besides God) could quickly impart those inner qualities. It would be cool to read a book on brokenness and then be broken (without having to endure the pain of life). I'd love to read a blog on integrity, then be totally like Christ. But spiritual shortcuts rarely work.

That's why it would be stupid for me to write a book guaranteeing "Three Steps to *It*." But here's what I can do. I can show you a few consistent qualities — that you *can* learn — that are almost always present when *it* is present. These are the qualities that I've observed are present in our *it*-rich campuses and missing in the *it*-poor campuses. And every *it*-ish church or ministry I've observed had these qualities. These are the qualities that I believe help contribute to *it*, or at least don't hinder *it*.

In part 2 of this book, we'll examine a few of the factors that seem to contribute to *it*. Some of our journey will be fun and encouraging. You'll have moments of celebration as God affirms that you've been following his lead. At other times, you may find yourself challenged — perhaps painfully so. You might even get mad at me. That's okay. That's all part of the journey to *it*. I hope to push you. Disturb you. Stretch you.

If you don't already see *it* in your ministry, perhaps *it* is closer than you think, bubbling just beneath the surface.

Maybe it's time to boil.

- *It* is not a model, system, or result of programs. You can't purchase *it*. *It* can't be copied. Not everyone will get *it*.
- *It* can't be learned. Even though *it* can't be taught, *it* can be caught.

FACTORS

Questions for Discussion or Reflection

1 *It* can be found in all types of churches. Do you agree or disagree? Why?

2 What *it* is not can be fairly obvious. What do you think are some ways of describing what *it* isn't?

3 In the next section of the book, we will discuss qualities that contribute to *it*. Before you look ahead, make a list of a few factors you think contribute to *it*.

4 What have you focused on that you thought would bring *it* but now you recognize won't? What can you do about it?

PART TWO

WHAT CONTRIBUTES TO it?

esterday I watched one of the top college football teams in the country. They won their tenth straight game — and won big, again. This team just might go undefeated. (Of course, with the BCS ranking system, they might not even qualify for a bowl game — but I'm not bitter.)

What makes for a great football team? Some might say, "It takes a great coach." That certainly helps. But without strong players, the coach can do only so much. Another person might argue, "The team needs a star quarterback." Again, that makes a difference. But without a good offensive line, the quarterback will never have time to throw. A third person might insist, "Defenses win games." Yes, a great defense is important. But the team still needs points on the board to walk away with a win.

Every championship team wins differently. Some win with a running game. Others with passing. Some are defensive giants. But no matter what the strategy, most winning teams have a few common ingredients. They have drive and desire. The players and coaches have a strong work ethic. They have good chemistry. They learn to win together.

The same is true in churches. Not every church can achieve *it* the same way. And they'd be foolish to try. Not every church will have a star preacher or the greatest worship leader. Not every church can afford a nice building. Not every church can bus in hundreds of kids to their youth ministry or host a large VBS.

But every ministry can develop some consistent qualities that contribute to *it*. In part 2, we'll examine several qualities you can pursue with your ministry leaders.

FOUR

VISION:

YOU CAN SEE it CLEARLY

> Worse than being blind would be to be able to see but not have any vision.
>
> —*Helen Keller*

this is a chapter about ... Just a minute while I check my notes ... Uh oh, I have no notes.

Well, I'm pretty sure this is the chapter about ... uh ... vision. Yeah, that sounds good. Vision.

Now, what can I come up with about vision? Besides what my optometrist told me last week. Oh, that reminds me. Gotta get a new plunger for the master bathroom. And flea treatment for the dog.

What? Oh, now where was I? Vision ...

One, two, three, four ... seventy-seven, seventy-eight. Wow, seventy-eight words already.

Now eighty-eight. Only 3,912 to go on this chapter. That shouldn't be too hard. Just keep typing, Craig.

Hmm. Let's see, what do I want to say next? I sure hope this chapter ends up somewhere good ...

Please Come Back!

Are you still reading?

I hope so, because I was joking. Trying to write a chapter with no direction — no vision for its purpose — would be disastrous. It would all add up to a huge waste of time for both of us.

But as silly as it sounds to write a chapter with no vision, think how foolish it would be to lead a church without vision.

I've met a lot of foolish leaders. I've been one.

The title of my first book, *Chazown*, is a Hebrew word that means "a dream, a revelation, or a vision." You can find *chazown* thirty-four times in the Old Testament. Proverbs 29:18 is the best-known verse containing *chazown*.

Look at how this Hebrew term in this verse is translated into English in some popular versions of the Bible:

"Where there is no *revelation*, the people cast off restraint" (NIV).

"Where there is no *vision*, the people perish" (KJV).

"When people do not accept *divine guidance*, they run wild" (NLT).

"Without *prophetic vision* people run wild" (God's Word).

"Where there is no *prophecy*, the people cast off restraint" (NRSV).

"If people can't see *what God is doing*, they stumble all over themselves" (MSG).

No matter how you translate it, without *chazown* (vision, revelation, divine guidance), the people we lead will be confused, scattered, unfocused, and easily distracted. Without a God-given vision, our ministries will never have *it*. Unfortunately, this is how many ministries and organizations function: visionless and without *it*.

Think of it this way: Have you ever driven a car with the wheels out of alignment? I do often because my wife is always hitting curbs and messing up our alignment. (We've got six kids. You try driving with half a dozen crazy children on board sometime!)

If you've ever driven a car with misaligned wheels, I'm sure you know what happens. Even though you try to keep the car in the middle of the road, it pulls to one side. It's a constant struggle to keep traveling in the intended direction. Over time, it can cause major problems. The tires wear out. And much worse, the poorly aimed wheels could pull you off the road into a crash.

People in a visionless church are like that. Without vision alignment, the people are busy doing *something*. They're driving along, doing church, but without any direction and are easily pulled off center. They're moving with no destination in mind.

Without a compelling vision, people, just like tires, quickly wear themselves out. Those who serve will burn out. Staff members will grow frustrated. Boards, elders, deacons, and leaders will disagree. (Have you ever witnessed a good old-fashioned deacons fight? It makes the movie *The Bourne Ultimatum* look slow and dull.) The ministry may have tons of activity, but there's little spiritual movement. And just like cars with misaligned wheels, ministries can crash.

Chase the Rabbit

Ministries that have *it* always have a clear vision. The people know the vision, understand the vision, believe in the vision, and live the vision. The vision guides them, motivates them, and energizes them. Large numbers of people move in the same direction. Ministries with vision tend to have *it*. All the rest are hit or miss.

It's a little like greyhound dog racing, a popular gambling sport. To keep the greyhounds running in the right direction, a man in the press box controls a mechanical rabbit, keeping it just in front of those dogs so they never quite catch it. They just chase it all the way around the track. Well, one time at a track in Florida, the man in the press box got ready to start the mechanical rabbit. All of the dogs were crouched in their cages. When he pushed the start button, the rabbit took off and the dogs took chase. But as the rabbit made the first turn, a short in the electrical system caused it to explode.

Suddenly the dogs didn't know what to do. There was no rabbit to chase, just a little piece of fur hanging on a wire. With the rabbit gone, some of the bewildered dogs plopped down on the track with their tongues hanging out. A couple of them tried to run through a fence and broke some ribs. The rest of the dogs just sat on the track and howled at the people in the stands. And not one dog finished the race.

Have you got teens in a small group who are like that? Or adults who serve on some church committee? Do you have anyone who is just plopped down in a pew with their tongue hanging out? Do you know someone causing damage by running off in their own direction? Do you have some members who are howling at the other people, creating problems by what they say, how they say it, what they disagree with? If so, maybe it's because they don't have a mechanical rabbit to chase. Without vision, people perish. Dreams fade. Youth groups lose their life. Once-vibrant churches slowly die. You need a clear vision that is constantly and enthusiastically cast.

Habakkuk 2:2 says, "And the Lord answered me and said, Write the vision and engrave it so plainly upon tablets that everyone who passes may [be able to] read [it easily and quickly] as he hastens by" (Amplified). Other translations say that this vision is supposed to be carried by a "runner" or a "herald," and it should be so clear, displayed so prominently, that people can see it and read it at a glance.

On the other hand, without a clear vision, a church or ministry can never expect to have *it*. Without a compelling vision, the organization is quickly pulled off center. People get confused, distracted, and bored. Without even noticing, the original mission fades as the organization drifts.

WHAT CONTRIBUTES TO **it?**

Years ago I went to a family reunion at the beach. After driving seventeen hours crammed in a minivan with a bunch of kids screaming "I've gotta go" and "Are we there yet?" we finally saw water, waves, and sand. Moments after unpacking the luggage, my kids and I dashed for the water. We were body surfing, floating on our backs, and singing the *Jaws* theme, pointing, and screaming, "Shark!"

After a long time of swimming, floating, and playing in the ocean, I looked toward shore for our beach lodging. I know you might not believe this, *but it was gone!* Vanished. The home was no longer there.

No, I wasn't smoking crack. Finally I realized that the house had moved way down the beach. Well, to be precise, *we* had moved. Without even realizing it, we had drifted.

That's what happens to churches. Without a consistent and compelling vision — constant orientation by fixed landmarks — they drift.

Keep the Vision Current

A ministry with a God-given and motivationally communicated vision typically gets *it*. But just because they have *it* doesn't mean they'll keep *it*. In fact, old vision is a lot like popcorn left out on the counter for three days. Have you ever tasted stale popcorn? The only thing worse is stale vision. If a ministry loses the vision (or even fulfills their old vision), it's only a matter of time before they lose what made them special in the first place. Without vision, the people will quickly lose *it*.

In my hometown, I watched a church that had a burning vision to pay off their debt. The whole church rallied around this vision. I'd never thought that a church could explode with growth around a debt-reduction campaign, but this one did. During this season of ministry, they had *it*. People were saved and baptized. Several hundred new people joined the church. They went from one service to two. They added staff. The members gave sacrificially and enthusiastically. People were pumped. This church had a compelling vision, a big goal in mind, and they attacked the goal passionately. They had *it*.

Several years later, this church successfully paid off several million dollars' worth of debt. Vision accomplished. Most would assume that *now* they were positioned to explode with growth. With all of the additional resources available to them, surely the ministry would soar like never before.

The opposite happened. No one had given much thought to what they'd do once they were out of debt. Now with more resources than ever, the leadership wondered what to do next. *Should we build a new building? Hire more staff? Maybe we should give money away. Or perhaps we should put some away in the bank for a rainy day.* So many options. So little vision.

Finally, after a year of stumbling around trying to find something to get excited about, the church initiated a building project. Midway through (believe it or not), they changed their plans, deciding to put the project on hold to start a different one.

Some people who had given money for the first project were confused and hurt. A few left the church. Within two short years, the church drifted from being healthy and vibrant to struggling and stagnant. The people didn't know what to do, what to get excited about, what to give their lives to. Still more people left. And the church that had grown around a vision started to die without one. When they had a vision, they had *it*. When they lost their vision, they lost *it*.

Define Your Vision

Do you have a vision? Many churches (and organizations) have a vision *statement*. But in reality, they have no vision. Just because you have words on a banner, a website, or a business card doesn't mean your leadership has a God-given vision. An idea is not a vision. Maybe you have an idea, but is it a God-inspired idea? There's a huge difference between a good idea and a God idea.

Without a vision, people become comfortable with the status quo. Later they grow to love the status quo. Eventually, they'll give their best to protect what *is*, never dreaming about what could or should be.

They need a vision with definition.

Here are some of the problems of the visionless ministry. When there is no vision:

- Most ideas seem like good ideas. This leads to over-programming and burnout.
- There is nothing compelling to give toward. This leads to a consumer mindset instead of a contributing mindset.
- Organizations become focused inward. This leads to a slow and painful death.
- Instead of working together, people compete for resources.

Many churches today are visionless. They've drifted. If you ask most church leaders, "What's your ministry about?" they'll give you a predictable response:

- "We're about loving God and loving people."
- "We're about reaching up and reaching out."
- "We're about preaching God's truth to set people free."
- "We're about teaching eternal truths in contemporary ways."
- "We exist to know Jesus and make him known."

If you look at what the ministry is *doing* and measure it against their claims, what you find is often inconsistent.

Here's a way to look at it. If a Martian came to visit earth ... (Work with me, okay?) Let's say that this is a CSI Martian who has come to investigate your church. (Still with me?) So he examines your church ... What would he think you're about?

Some churches would look like a sort of entertainment business. People come, watch the show, put their money in a bucket, then leave.

Some churches would look more like a self-help facility. Find out how to fix your marriage, raise your kids, manage your money, and make good decisions.

Some churches would look like a country club. Dress in your best clothes. Pay your dues. Check out who's there and make sure everyone sees you.

Obviously these examples are extreme. But if our CSI Martian knew nothing about your vision and observed everything you do all week long, what would he conclude? And would he say, "That church is all about someone named Jesus"?

Finding the Vision

Years ago, I was part of a ministry that formed a committee of forty people determined to discover the church's five-year vision. This brave group of laypeople interviewed dozens of church members. Everyone shared their great ideas. After months of listening, dreaming, and planning, guess what happened? To put it simply, the vision became "Let's do everything."

I'm not joking. This midsized church decided to do just about every good thing you could ever think of ... and more. The committee decided to have car-care ministry, busing ministry, elderly ministry, single adults ministry, Sunday school ministry, Wednesday night Bible study, small groups ministry, shut-ins ministry, quilting ministry, ministry to business professionals, music lessons ministry, handbell choir outreach ministry, a day care, daily devotions, a radio ministry, a choir internship, reading club ministry, and a floss-the-teeth-of-elderly-shut-ins ministry. Okay, I made up that last one. But all the rest were real, and I could add more to the list.

Hopefully, the *leaders* of your church will seek God, find a divine burden, examine their resources and context, and present a Spirit-breathed, God-sized vision! Notice that I italicized the word *leaders*. If you're the leader of a ministry, this is *your* role. This certainly doesn't mean that you won't listen to people, seeking their wisdom and input. But ultimately, the vision comes from the leaders' time of hearing from God.

Here are a few questions to stir your vision. (You might want to jot down some answers. Or maybe your team could explore these questions together.)

1. Why does your organization exist? (If you can't answer this clearly, I'll bet you an overpriced latte that there are a few things your organization should *stop* doing immediately.)
2. What can your organization be the best in the world at? (Borrowing from Jim Collins in *Good to Great*.)

WHAT CONTRIBUTES TO it?

3. If you could do only one thing, what would it be?
4. If you left your organization tomorrow, what would you hope would continue forever?
5. What breaks your heart, keeps you awake at night, wrecks you?

An Effective Vision

As God gives you clarity, you'll want to work hard to communicate this vision. One of my mentors, Dr. Sam Chand, always says, "An effective vision will always be memorable, portable, and motivational."[1]

A great vision statement is *memorable*. If people can't remember your vision, your church will never have *it*.

Have you ever seen a mission statement like this? "We exist to reach as many people as possible in our city for Jesus Christ before he returns for his bride, the church, by loving them, accepting them, teaching them God's uncompromised Word and empowering them through Spirit-filled discipleship to become fully devoted Christ-followers, reaching up, reaching in, reaching out, and building people to exalt, edify, and equip the saints of God to go into all the world and make disciples of all nations, baptizing them in the name of the Father, and the Son, and the Holy Spirit, for the glory of our God, who reigns forever and ever. Amen."

The only thing memorable about that is the number of breaths it took to say it. You want a vision statement that's easy to remember. Short is better. Make it crisp. Make it clear. Make it memorable.

Your vision must also be *portable*. In other words, people must be able to take it with them and easily communicate it to others. You'll want everyone on your staff and everyone in the church to be able to give the "vision pitch." In less than one minute, everyone in your organization should be able to describe what you're about.

One of the greatest compliments I've received as a leader was from my friend Lyle Schaller. When he visited our church, he met with staff members at every level in the organization. I remember him smiling as he said, "Craig, your team is brainwashed." I stared at him, somewhat concerned. Lyle laughed and said, "They're brainwashed in the best way possible. Everyone — and I mean *everyone!* — knows the vision and wants to help fulfill it." Your vision needs mobility. Make sure it's portable.

Not only should the vision be memorable and portable but it should also be *motivational.* If your vision doesn't compel people, move people, stir people, your vision is too small. Your vision must be something that burns in your heart but is too big for you to do on your own. If you could do it, then you wouldn't need God. The vision should capture attention, stir hearts, and be irresistibly moving. It should cause agitation, ambition, ignition, even competition.

It tends to follow big vision. Here are some benefits of vision:

- People tend to give sacrificially for it (both financially and of themselves).
- People will tolerate inconveniences for the greater cause.
- People will talk. You cannot put a price tag on positive buzz.
- The organization (or ministry) will take on a life of its own.
- Opportunities for distraction will decrease.

You'll want to communicate the vision — over and over again. My friend Bill Hybels said, "You can never underestimate the amount of energy and frequency you must give to vision casting. You can never underestimate it."[2] Just when you think you've thoroughly explained the vision, it's time to start over and communicate it all again.

Hybels says, "Vision leaks." I wholeheartedly believe that you'd be hard pressed to overcommunicate your vision. One school of thought suggests that as soon as you decide that you've been talking about it too much, that's actually when it's just beginning to stick with people. Talk about the vision. Tell stories about the vision. Illustrate the vision. Reward those who live the vision. Highlight the vision anywhere you see it. Once you've done all of the above, do it all again.

Here are a few of the things we do to move the vision forward:

- We produce simple vodcasts and email them to members and attenders to renew the vision of the church.

- We share video testimonies with the church to celebrate how the vision is changing lives.
- We preach two series a year that help renew the passion for the vision.
- When ministry attempts don't work well, we use failure as a teaching time on how we can better fulfill the vision.
- We gather all the volunteers for an annual vision renewal and time of celebration.
- We invite every attender to invest their lives toward the vision every January.

Ministries that have *it* have big vision that bears constant repetition!

Three Levels of Vision Buy-In

Those ministries that have *it* are filled with people who understand and believe in the vision. Ministries without *it* are made up of people who might like the ministry but don't understand where it is going.

In my experience, I've discovered three levels of vision buy-in. Ministries without *it* have people at levels one and two. Ministries with *it* tend to have more and more people moving to level three.

Level 1: The people believe in the vision enough to benefit from it. Like the person who benefits from the service at their favorite restaurant or works out at the conveniently located gym, these church attenders are people with a consumer mindset. They come to church because they like it. They receive something from the ministry. And to them, that's what's important.

Level 2: The people believe in the vision enough to contribute comfortably. Like the person who drops some change in a Muscular Dystrophy Association jar or participates in a Neighborhood Watch program, these are people who were consumers but are ready to contribute as long as it's easy. They're happy to help if it doesn't interfere with their other priorities.

Level 3: The people believe in the vision enough to give their lives to it. These are the people who understand the vision and get *it*. They recognize that their lives are not their own. They belong to Jesus. They are a part of the greatest cause on earth.

Everyone craves a cause to fight for. We love to be part of something that is making a difference. As leaders, it's our role to seek God, see the vision, communicate it in a compelling way, and invite people to give their lives for the greatest cause on earth — the cause of Christ.

See It and Create It

The legendary Walt Disney died before Disney World in Florida was completed. On opening day in 1971, almost five years after Disney's death, someone commented to Mike Vance, creative director of Walt Disney Studios, "Isn't it too bad Walt Disney didn't live to see this?"

"He did see it," Vance replied simply. "That's why it's here."

Seek God. Hear from God. Receive his vision. Let it overwhelm you. Consume you. Burden you. Tell the vision. Cast the vision. Communicate the vision. And watch *it* spread.

- Without a vision, the people will never get *it* and keep *it*.
- *It* doesn't show up on its own. *It* follows big vision.
- The vision must be memorable, portable, and motivational.
- You can't overcommunicate vision!

 FACTORS

Questions for Discussion or Reflection

1 Proverbs 29:18 says, "Where there is no vision, the people perish." Describe an area of your ministry that is struggling because it lacks vision.

2 Can you pinpoint an area (or areas) in which your ministry has drifted from your vision? What do you need to do to pull it back to the center?

3 Can you clearly define your vision? Why does your ministry exist? Don't skim over these questions. You may want to put the book aside and pray for some time. Make sure you can answer this before you go on. What has God uniquely prepared and equipped your ministry to accomplish?

4 There are three levels of vision buy-in. Some believe in the vision enough to benefit from it. Others believe in it enough to contribute comfortably. Ideally, people believe in the vision enough to give their lives to it. What percentage of your staff team is at the third level? What about the people in your ministry? What can you do to increase the number of those who will give their lives for God's work?

WHAT CONTRIBUTES TO it?

PROFILE

Herbert Cooper

People's Church

Oklahoma City, Oklahoma

> *Vision leaks, so share it over and over and over again. If you don't some-times feel like you're sharing it too much, you're not sharing it enough.*
>
> —HERB COOPER

Herbert and Tiffany Cooper moved from Springfield, Missouri, to Oklahoma City and launched People's Church in 2002. On May 12, 2002, the church had its grand opening with sixty-five people meeting in a rented movie theater. Because the church was built on a strong God-given vision, five years later two thousand people call People's Church their home.

When I asked Herb what he believes God wants to accomplish through his ministry, he boldly described a future church with twenty thousand attenders and two thousand small groups. Without taking a breath, Herb explained that People's Church will one day start a daughter church or a new campus each year while giving over one million dollars annually to missions.

Behind all of these numbers is Herb's real passion. Because Herb is black and is married to a white woman, his family has a burden for building a multicultural church. Herb says with passion, "Diversity is celebrated. Every person is invaluable and irreplaceable. The eth-nic, social, and religious distinctions that divide society disappear in Christ. Our differences become our strengths. People's Church is a unique atmosphere where *all* people connect with God."

People's Church is on track to accomplish this vision. Anyone you talk to who has been at the church for any length of time will recite the same vision. I asked Herb to unpack his strategy. He explained that while many pastors present an annual vision message, Herb preaches four each year. The balance of the year, Herb weaves the vision into everything. He'll show videos during messages and announcements to reinforce the vision. He leverages his daily blog to share the vision. He publicly and privately rewards those who advance the vision.

Herb knows that infusing the staff with a constant dose of vision is essential to a vision-driven church. Each month, his entire staff enjoys a gathering devoted solely to celebrating the advancement of the vision with stories, testimonies, and prayer. Herb is famous for quickly redirecting a staff member who slightly drifts from the vision, and he meets with staff members individually for the sole purpose of infecting them with the church vision.

I asked Herb what advice he'd give a pastor whose church has lost the vision. Herb gave six powerful suggestions. If a ministry has vision drift, a wise leader should:

- Pray and fast like crazy while asking God to reignite the vision.
- Pull together the key leaders to help them catch the vision.
- Preach a series of messages to get the church "jazzed up" about the vision.
- Have faith in God and start taking steps to see the vision come to pass.
- Stop doing things that aren't accomplishing the vision or moving the church toward seeing the vision fulfilled.
- Reallocate funds in the church budget to accomplish the vision.

Herb says, "You can't ever share the vision enough. Many people will forget the vision an hour after you share it, so share it again and again and again. People are attracted to and motivated by a God-sized vision. A God-sized vision unifies a church, attracts resources, motivates volunteers, and unites strong leaders. Sharing the God-sized vision is one of the most important jobs of the pastor."

FIVE

DIVINE FOCUS:

YOU KNOW WHERE it IS NOT

Most people have no idea of the great capacity we can immediately command when we focus all of our resources on mastering a single area of our lives.

—Anthony Robbins

have you ever seen a Magic Eye picture? At first glance, it looks like a pattern of colors that amounts to ... well ... nothing. Unless you can attain visual breakthrough.

For years I'd been told that if you focus *just* right, these collages will reveal hidden three-dimensional pictures that will take your breath away. And I hated everyone who told me that. I never saw squat. Some told me the trick was to not really look at the picture. Others told me to stare deeply *into* the picture. Still others exhorted me to look *through* the picture. (Whatever that means.) I decided the trick might be to OD on cold medicine before even approaching the picture.

Then finally *my* day arrived. Pumped full of the determination of Jacob as he wrestled with the angel of God, I decided

I'd stare at the picture until Christ returned or I saw the 3-D picture — whichever came first.

I stared. And stared. And stared some more. I tried not really looking at it, staring deeply into it, and looking through it. I squinted. I crossed my eyes. I closed my eyes and believed the Force was with me. The clock ticked slowly. Nothing. I continued to stare, calling upon God for his visual blessing. Tick. Tick. Tick.

Then it happened. For an instant, I saw it! Sweet mystery of life, at last I've found you! Three-dimensional dolphins jumped off the page. *Flipper, I love you!*

For a brief and glorious moment, God smiled on me. Then as quickly as it came, I lost the vision and it became blurry again. I still hate those stupid pictures.

Business consultant Nido Qubein says, "Nothing can add more power to your life than concentrating all your energies on a limited set of targets." The apostle Paul showed his focus when he said, "But *one thing* I do: Forgetting what is behind and straining toward what is ahead, I press on toward the goal to win the prize for which God has called me heavenward in Christ Jesus" (Phil. 3:13 – 14, emphasis mine).

In my observation, ministries that have *it* tend to be focused on a limited set of targets. They do a few things as if all eternity hinged on their results, and they do these things with godly excellence. They clearly see the vision and drive toward it with laser-guided precision. Those who have *it* know what they are called to do and what they are not called to do. Their vision is characterized by specificity. Selectivity. Exclusivity.

Focused ministries often wake up and discover that God is doing something special in their midst — they have *it*. They're almost obnoxiously passionate about a few important things. Their passion and effectiveness attract the right leaders. The right leaders use their gifts and give their lives to make a difference. And God blesses them with *it* — his mysteriously awesome presence, power, and peace.

It's interesting to me that when a ministry is faithful and one day wakes up and has *it* — that impossible to describe presence and power of God — they're often blinded by their success. Instead of seeing with the crystal-clear vision that helped attract *it*, they find that their vision begins to blur. Instead of being clear, their vision becomes clouded. Instead of focusing on the main thing, the leaders become distracted. The very thing that God blessed — obedience to his specific calling — is one of the first things successful ministries unknowingly abandon. The story is all too common.

The first time I was part of a ministry with *it* was in college. A few of my party friends and I stumbled into starting a small Bible study. Did I say Bible study? It was actually about eight or ten of us who gathered — before going out drinking — to read a chapter of the Bible and pray that God would protect us as we partied. But God was up to something. One by one, he was drawing us to himself. God quickly and dramatically redirected our lives toward pleasing him.

Through that small group of students, God lit a spark that spread to hundreds across the campus, and I was one of the ones who caught the fire. As one of the newest believers, and certainly one of the most excited (and obnoxious), I was thrust into becoming one of the two leaders of the group. With zero Bible knowledge, zero ministry experience, and nothing more than simple passion for the one who'd just changed my life, I attacked the campus with the love of Christ like I'd never attacked anything in my life.

Because we'd come to Christ as a result of reading the Bible, our focus was simple. Get people to read the Bible. That was it. Nothing more. Nothing less. Our goal was to get anyone and everyone to gather and we'd read God's Word. No group was ever more naive than we were. If the Bible said it, we believed it was possible.

When the Bible said God would answer our prayers, we prayed — and he answered our prayers. When the Bible said to pray for those who were sick, we prayed — and God often healed the sick. When the Bible said to sell something and give the money to the poor, we did just that. When the Bible said we were the salt and light of the world, we took that direction and told everyone we knew about Jesus.

God gave *it* to our little Bible study. As more people all around us read God's Word, they seemed to get *it*. And *it* was one of the most special works of God I'd ever seen.

People were saved. Lots of them. Athletes came to Christ. Professors were baptized. Sorority girls left keg parties to pray. One girl who had really bad eyesight was healed. Everyone on this small campus knew something was happening. The word spread, and so did *it*.

This little band of non-seminary-trained, immature, but sincerely passionate people experienced the kinds of things you read about in the book of Acts. God had given us *it* — his extra dose of real, sincere, Spirit-filled life and power. And it was more special than I can describe.

This ministry grew so quickly and so large that the leaders of the college took notice. Since we weren't an official organization and we were causing quite a stir, we were politely — well, actually not so politely — asked to meet off campus. Nothing like the working of God to threaten the establishment.

If you asked us what we were about, we would've told you, "All we do is read the Bible and do what it says." And that was it. We had a divine focus.

Then one day, someone had a good idea.

Notice I said a good idea, not a God idea. The idea sounded logical. It made sense. It seemed like a natural step in a growing ministry. Little did we know that this one small suggestion was the beginning of our losing what had helped bring *it* — divine focus. Someone once said, "If you chase two rabbits, both will escape." As we chased a new rabbit, little did we know that this one idea quietly and subtly lured us away from the heart of our ministry. It was the beginning of our losing focus on what we were about, and the first step we took toward losing *it*.

What was the idea? It wasn't something weird, strange, or inherently dangerous. No one brought a bag of poisonous snakes to handle. No one started voodoo chants or drinking poisoned Kool-Aid. And no one decided we should all intermarry, build a rocket ship, fly to another planet, and start a new and supernaturally charged race of people.

The idea was a bake sale. To raise money.

That was it. Well-meaning Christians have been doing it since the invention of the oven. Bake something. Find a table. Write prices on poster board. Sit there all day. And raise $34.50 selling goodies to anyone who'll buy them. It's always been the same (except for a few years in the sixties when the brownies contained a special ingredient). It seemed like there was nothing dangerous about our doing a bake sale. It was something incredibly small. It just wasn't at the core of who God had called us to be.

As I reflect, I'm not sure why we thought we needed money. We didn't have any expenses. We didn't even take an offering every week. Money originally wasn't even on our radar. But other ministries raised money, so why not?

That was the beginning of the blur.

For the first time ever, we had some money to spend. Someone suggested we use it to take a few people on a leadership and planning retreat. We'd brainstorm. We'd plan. We'd dream up some ways to make the ministry really great (ignoring that it was already special). And that's when our vision blurred and we compromised our focus.

On our brainstorming getaway, someone suggested we start taking a weekly offering. Another person recommended we all do a mission trip to Mexico. Another person proposed that we pay one of the volunteers a small salary because she was working hard and was in need. Two others thought we should take our ministry to high schools. That led to a suggestion that we form a team of traveling speakers. Another was convinced we were supposed to turn the Bible study into a church.

Over the next few months, we tried all those ideas and more. Sadly, we'd taken our eyes off the target. The one thing that God was blessing was helping others to know him through his Word. And we took attention away from that one thing and added dozens of other things — and wondered why over the next few months we were losing *it*.

I'm not suggesting that expanding or doing new things is wrong. But you can't overestimate the power of focus. Motivational speaker Anthony Robbins once said, "One reason so few of us achieve what we truly want is that we never direct our focus; we never concentrate our power. Most people dabble their way through life, never deciding to master anything in particular."[3] Doing the wrong new things, things that usurp what God calls us to do, is dangerous. Focus tends to let *it* breathe. Lack of focus generally suffocates *it*.

Too Many, Too Much, Too Bad

In Luke 10, Martha was overwhelmed with all of the responsibilities of hosting Jesus. While she was doing everything possible, Mary simply sat at Jesus' feet. Martha complained to Jesus, asking him to tell Mary to help her. " 'Martha, Martha,' the Lord answered, 'you are worried and upset about many things, but only *one thing* is needed. Mary has chosen what is better, and it will not be taken away from her' " (Luke 10:41 – 42, emphasis mine). To have *it*, you'll have to choose not to do everything. Those who attempt to do everything always lose *it*.

An Italian proverb says, "Often he who does too much does too little." (Smart people, huh? No wonder they're called *It*alians.) Too many ministries are doing too little by doing too much. For example, a lot of pastors boast about how many ministries they have in their church. The other day I met a guy with a church of about four hundred people (with a staff of eight) who told me he had 187 different ministries in his church. I didn't know if he was bragging, asking me to pray for him, or making the case for a frontal lobotomy.

I could hardly get my mind around what he said. *One hundred and eighty-seven ministries!* Trying hard not to reveal my shock, I asked which ones were the most important and effective. Smiling sincerely, he said, "All of them." Then he said that they hoped to start many more.

His church is smaller this year than it was last year, and last year it was smaller than the year before. To me, this doesn't sound like a focused vision. It sounds like ministry schizophrenia. (The

WHAT CONTRIBUTES TO **it**?

voices are telling me to start a new ministry ... I must start a new ministry.)

Jim Collins in his book *Good to Great* referenced the ancient Greek parable of "The Fox and the Hedgehog." Day after day, the cunning fox plans his attack on the unsuspecting hedgehog. No matter how creative the fox is, the hedgehog always wins. Why? The fox knows many things, but the hedgehog knows one big thing. Each time the fox attacks, the hedgehog simply rolls up into a ball of sharp spikes, creating an impenetrable defense. It's what he does best.

That brings us back to Collins' question, which we encountered in the last chapter: what can you be the best in the world at? In ministry terms, what do you do best? If you could do only one thing in ministry, what would you do? Think about that. Wrestle with the question. Allow it to consume your thoughts. Read the question again and don't move on until you can answer it with confidence: if you could do only one thing in ministry, what would you do?

The To-Don't List

If you *aren't* interested in having *it*, take on a lot of ministries. The more a church does, the less likely they are to have *it*. Why? Because it's impossible to have 187 *effective* ministries in one church. It's challenging to have three very effective ministries.

Many great businesses understand this principle. One example is In-N-Out Burger. Not only is their food delicious, but the chain is also very profitable. They offer only a few items. In fact, I just pulled up their website and it said, "Ordering as easy as 1, 2, 3." They offered me three choices:

1. The Double-Double with fries and a drink
2. The Cheeseburger with fries and a drink
3. The Hamburger with fries and a drink

In-N-Out Burger knows burgers, fries, and drinks. Notice they're not selling waffles, lattes, or taco salads with guacamole. They're not offering 187 different kinds of burgers. They're offering just three. They're a hedgehog. (How they keep the bristly hairs out of their food, I'll never know.)

Instead of thinking about what you want to add to your ministry to-do list, maybe you should pray about what to add to your ministry to-don't list. Some call it planned abandonment. You are planning what things you won't do, that most do, to do best what God called you to do. (Did that make sense? If not, read it again slowly.) To be great at a few things and experience *it*, you'll have to say no to many things.

You might need a conjunction change.

Do you remember the song "Conjunction Junction" from *Schoolhouse Rock*? (It was the one that played right before "I'm Just a Bill." Sorry to date myself like that.) Maybe you need a conjunction change that could drastically improve your ministry. Most people say "and" much of the time. We need to say "or" most of the time. For example, instead of saying, "We can do a singles ministry *and* a counseling ministry *and* a sports ministry *and* missions *and* divorce care *and* a puppet ministry *and* a quilting ministry *and* a ministry for people being stalked by their imaginary girlfriends," we need to say, "We can do this *or* that and do it well. We can't do it all. Let's focus on what God is calling us to do."

Cutting Back to Move Forward

In the last chapter, we talked about the importance of vision. Don't let your vision become blurry. Busyness blurs ministry vision. Instead of planting more ministries under your direct care, maybe you need to consider pruning the ministry vine.

Thom Rainer and Eric Geiger, in their book *Simple Church*, define focus as "the commitment to abandon everything that falls outside of the simple ministry process."[4] Following their definition, ask yourself, What are we doing that doesn't directly contribute to our vision in a high-impact way? Think about it. Be honest. Let me ask you the question again. This is too important to miss. What are you doing that isn't directly contributing with high impact to your vision? The answer to that question needs to be eliminated.

Gasp.

I can feel you shudder. Your blood pressure is rising. You might be thinking, *If I kill that ministry, what will the people do?*

You're imagining the gossip.

You see dozens of people leaving the church.

You're reading the negative blogs about you.

You visualize yourself delivering pizza for a living.

You see your head deacon holding one of your children hostage until you reinstate his wife's sewing ministry.

I acknowledge that cutting a ministry can be traumatic. But as with any life-saving surgery, it nevertheless needs to be done.

Or you might simply take a break from a particular activity. Yesterday I had a conversation with pastor Rick Warren. For years and years, Saddleback Church has impacted thousands of leaders through Purpose Driven conferences. After praying faithfully, Rick and his team decided not to do any conferences this year. Instead of conferences, they're having conversations. Rick is spending the year interacting with other leaders rather than teaching them.

I heard about one church that suspended all of its ministries (except weekend worship) for the summer. At the end of the summer, they restarted only the few that they believed truly contributed to the vision.

Pruning Our Ministry Vine

Let me tell you part of our church's story to illustrate. We were a church that grew slowly in the early years. For the first few years, I never felt like we were a real church. In my warped mind, I believed we needed our own building and all the other things real churches have — like a sports ministry, concerts, conferences, and our own church van. I thought those important elements would give us *it*. Then we'd be a real church.

Little did I realize, we already had *it*. God was doing something very special. Lost people were being found. Found people were growing. The church was spiritually vibrant. All without any of the things I thought necessary.

One day we built the building I'd dreamed about. A little later, we started the sports ministry that I just knew was necessary. Before long we held a real concert with tickets and overpriced, low-quality T-shirts for sale. Then we hosted a marriage conference featuring a well-known speaker who had his own radio show. Eventually, we even bought our very own van so our students could play Truth or Dare in the back while driving home from camp. (At least that's what I used to do.)

We had arrived! Legitimacy at last.

Then one day I realized that everything I'd always wanted was slowly killing everything we already had. Our church had *it* and we didn't know it. So we added things we didn't need and strangled what we already had. All these new things that we finally started doing didn't contribute to the vision. They competed with the vision. We were directing tons of resources into nonproductive areas.

Finally I recognized the insanity of it all. I looked at the sports ministry and realized that we were taking Christians out of their work leagues with non-Christians so they could play together (and act like non-Christians). How stupid was that?

Our concerts cost us a ton of money and even more time and effort basically to entertain Christians who went to other churches. Stupid again.

Another time we spent ten thousand dollars to bring in one of the best marriage-conference guys, but only eight couples showed up. Stupid on steroids.

And one of the tires on our van blew out on the highway, rolling the van and throwing several people out on the side of the road. (No one was killed or permanently injured. Praise God for his protection.)

That's when I decided that we didn't need the sports ministry, concerts, conferences, or a church van. And we could still be a real church. In fact, after more time in prayer, our leaders decided to cut all but five ministry activities. To this day, we do only five things. Five is not set in stone. Someday we might cut it down to three or maybe bump it up to six. But as of today, it's five.

WHAT CONTRIBUTES TO **it?**

What are the five things we do? We focus all of our energy on:

1. Weekend experiences
2. Missions
3. Small Groups
4. Kids
5. Students

That's it.

But what about Sunday school? What about Wednesday night Bible study? Vacation Bible school?

My answer: no.

What about singles ministry? Men's ministry? Women's ministry?

No again.

What about church conferences? Apologetics conferences? Financial management conferences?

Again … no.

Christmas pageants? Easter productions? Children's musicals?

Absolutely not.

To some of you, I just became a heretic. Others might think I'm a hero with superpowers.

We do five things. Why? Because we believe those are the five things that God has called us to do and has best equipped us to do. Just because you *can* do something doesn't mean you *should* do it.

A Great Work

When Nehemiah was faithfully rebuilding the broken walls of Jerusalem, two of his enemies, Sanballat and Geshem, invited him to a meeting to thwart his progress. We need to commit Nehemiah's response to memory. The NLT words it this way: "So I replied by sending this message to them: 'I am doing a *great work!* I cannot stop to come and meet with you'" (Neh. 6:3, emphasis mine).

Nehemiah had *it*. And the people with him had *it*. (Can you imagine the thrill of working with people you love serving the God of heaven and making history? In the next chapter, we'll examine how this type of camaraderie contributes to *it*.) The people were working together, empowered by God and great leadership, and they were accomplishing the impossible.

Those who have *it* stick with what brings *it*. When you know you're doing a great work, do your best not to be distracted. If you have *it*, guard *it*. Don't distort *it* by doing the wrong things. When you increase your focus, you decrease your options. Good things are not necessarily God things.

- Those who do it all tend to lose *it*.
- The clearer your vision becomes, the easier it is to guard what God calls you to do.
- Instead of saying "and," maybe you need to say "or."
- If you chase two rabbits, both will escape.
- To be great at a few things and experience *it*, you'll have to say no to many things.
- When focus increases, options decrease.
- Those who have *it* stick with what brings *it*.

it FACTORS

WHAT CONTRIBUTES TO **it**?

Questions for Discussion or Reflection

1 Jim Collins writes about the "hedgehog principle." Look carefully at the people God has put around you, the resources you have available to you, and the people who are within reach of your ministry and answer this question: what can we be the best in the world at?

2 Good can be the enemy of the great. As you narrow in on what you can do great, what good things on your to-do list need to be switched to your to-don't list?

3 Most churches add and add and add ministries to their organizations. Maybe it's time to "prune the vine." If you had to remove one part of your ministry today, what would it be?

4 What few ministries are necessary to fulfilling your vision? If you could do only a few things for the greatest ministry return, what things you would do?

PROFILE

Mark Driscoll
Mars Hill Church
Seattle, Washington

> *We cannot say Jesus' name often enough, preach Jesus' gospel passionately enough, or sing Jesus' praises loudly enough.*
>
> — MARK DRISCOLL

In 1996, Mark Driscoll started a church in one of the most unchurched cities in America. Seattle, Washington, is known to have more dogs than Christians. In one of the most challenging cultures to reach, Mars Hill Church, through focused preaching of God's Word, has grown from a handful of people to over seven thousand people meeting in six locations across Seattle.

Mars Hill's growth shows no sign of slowing. One of the many impressive qualities of this ministry is its single-minded focus. If I had to use only one word to describe the focus of Driscoll's ministry, that word would unquestionably be *Jesus*. When I asked Mark the secret of his ministry's growth, he said, "The key is the preaching of the person and work of Jesus Christ from the Bible every week with passion and clarity. The issue is always, only, fully, clearly, uncompromisingly, and exclusively Jesus. If Jesus is lifted up, then a crowd will gather, that crowd will be converted, those converts will become passionate, that passion will result in creativity, and that creativity will result in a movement of God, because the Holy Spirit delights to work through his people to the glory of Jesus."

Driscoll explains, "In the past, the big ate the small, so the key was to grow a large church with a lot of programming and complexity. In the present, the fast eat the slow, so the key is to grow a nimble church of flexible teams and only essential programming." That's why Mars Hill aborts any ministry that's not working. Their motto is, "Jesus is the only thing that we promise will never change."

Mark and his leaders refuse to plan too far into the future. Over-planning could lead to trusting in programs instead of trusting in Jesus. By planning only a quarter in advance, the leaders can better assess the spiritual viability of a ministry to determine if its short-term future is secure. If the ministry isn't producing fruit, Mars Hill will shut it down.

Mark explains that past successes often hinder future successes. In some churches, what worked last year becomes enshrined as sacred. Not at Mars Hill. Mark teaches, "One key to pastoral leadership is knowing when to shoot your dogs and how to shoot them well so they don't come back to bite you. We decided not to let sick dogs live and as a result have a lot of shell casings lying around."

Most would admit that many churches are doing too much. Mark advises the wise leader to do well one thing at a time. Instead of focusing on ten, fifteen, or forty areas of ministry, ask God what he has uniquely created you and positioned you to do. Then pursue that one calling with divine passion.

When you succeed at one thing, Mark explains, you can build your ministry from success. The small victories help create momentum for the church and builds trust with the people. This spiritual progress can build on itself.

Mark believes the first priority should be the Sunday service, since it is the most public and visible aspect of the church. After that, the website should be the next priority, along with small groups. In this way, the website becomes the front door, the Sunday service becomes the living room, and the small groups become the dinner table for the church family.

At Mars Hill, Driscoll and the leaders are focused on getting Jesus to men. Mark says, "If you get the men, you win the war. If you get the young men, you also win the war for the future." He explains that there are between eleven and thirteen million more Christian women than Christian men. Sixty percent of Christians are female. He expresses excitement over the number of women who are followers of Christ, while sounding the alarm that most churches are not attracting, converting, and deploying godly, gifted, competent Christian men. When I asked Mark what else he would like to add, he said, "If I had three final suggestions, they would be get the men, get the men, get the men."

SIX

UNMISTAKABLE CAMARADERIE:

YOU ENJOY *it* WITH OTHERS

It is better to have one person working with you than three people working for you.

—*Dwight D. Eisenhower*

did you see the movie *Jerry Maguire*? The title character, played by Tom Cruise, helped manage the careers of professional athletes. Toward the end of the movie, after one of those rare emotional guy moments, Jerry tightly embraced his client and friend Rod Tidwell (played by Cuba Gooding Jr.). Another athlete observed this with envy and disappointment and asked his agent, "Why don't we hug like that?" The agent (a money-grabbing jerk) hesitated, then — you could almost see him thinking, *The things I do for a buck* — turned and reached for an embrace. The two men stopped midhug and pulled apart awkwardly.

It wasn't working.

No Faking *It*

Ministries that have *it* enjoy *it* together. They have an unmistakable camaraderie. Anyone close to them can see *it*. They can feel *it*. Affinity, community, sincerity, fraternity (and sorority). Christianity at its best. The people love being together. And when they are, when the people interact, *it* is electric.

For the church to have *it*, the staff (or volunteers) will likely have *it* first. As it goes with the leaders, so it goes with the whole organization. While I'd love to devote time to talking about community in the whole church family, I'll limit the discussion to the staff and volunteers. This is what I'll refer to as "the team."

To have *it* everywhere, *it* has to start somewhere. *It* must begin with your team.

Friendships matter. Studies reveal just how important friendships at work are to *it*. Gallup research shows that close friendships at work boost employee satisfaction by almost 50 percent.[5] Tom Rath, global practice leader at Gallup, explains why employees who have a best friend at work are seven times more likely to be emotionally engaged on the job. He says, "People with friends at work are 96 percent more likely to be extremely satisfied with their life." Happier people make better team members. Yet he reports that fewer than one in five people consider their boss to be a close friend. But when a team member is close to the boss, she is two and a half times more likely to be satisfied on the job.[6]

On our staff, our longest-tenured members are my closest friends. Brian Bruss started when our church was five months old and he had barely reached puberty. (Just kidding, Brian. I know you had already reached puberty. I meant to say you *acted* like you had barely reached puberty.) Lanita Lukens began around the same time. She was the most conservative person I'd ever met. Now she can crack jokes with the best of them. My assistant and friend, Sarah, has served with me for more than six years. (I knew she'd be great when I was interviewing her for the job. I was unaware that someone had hidden a fart machine in the conference room. When the machine ripped a couple of rounds off during the interview, Sarah busted out laughing and said that was nothing compared to her husband. She fit right in.) Mark Dawson is our head video guy. He's one of the closest friends I have. (And I can never betray him because he can make my nose look bigger on-screen than it already is.) Kevin, Bobby, Jerry, and Sam are the directional leaders at our church. When we get together, we laugh so hard we cry. (Except for Kevin, who is our senior member. He simply wets his pants.) All of these team members would tell you that a big part of their ministry satisfaction are the fun and memories we share together.

The team with *it* loves each other. Not only do they minister together, they do life together. What they have is more than friendship. It's something that God gives — more of a partnership of people with deep love committed to a single mission. You're more than friends. You're a team.

Have you heard of the book with the memorable title *Refrigerator Rights*? In it, authors Will Miller and Glenn Sparks talk about how few people today have these rights in each other's lives.

You're probably wondering, *What are refrigerator rights?* Someone with refrigerator rights is a person who is so trusted that they can walk into your home, open your refrigerator, and help themselves to a sandwich and a drink. They don't have to ask. (*Mi casa, su casa* and my bologna sandwich is your bologna sandwich.)

If you're like most people, I suspect that very few people have refrigerator rights in your home. Most people are too busy to really get to know each other.

People may have friends at work or at the gym or at PTA meetings, but few do life together in their homes.

By contrast, teams with *it* are so connected and committed to each other, they almost always have refrigerator rights. When someone else sees *it*, they look on with envy. *Why don't we hug like that? Why can't I open your refrigerator and make myself a bologna sandwich with Dijon mustard and cheese? Why can't I borrow a pair of your boxers?*

But just as the jerk agent in *Jerry Maguire* couldn't fake a hug, you can't fake this kind of bond. Not every ministry team has *it*. Most don't. And *its* absence is as obvious as *its* presence in a team. Instead of humming with a relational buzz, a room of *it*-less people is mostly silent. When they do talk, it's all business. Little laughter, little joy, little life. They work together, but they don't share *it* together.

What's the Problem?

Pollster George Barna conducted an interesting study which revealed that 92 percent of Americans claim to be independent.[7] For many people, independence is a goal. A virtue. They want to be financially independent — *I don't need to depend on anyone for money.* They want to be professionally independent — *I don't report to anyone.* And they want to be relationally independent — *I don't need anyone or answer to anyone.*

A business woman wants to believe she's a self-made woman. Many athletes are more concerned with their own performance than with the results of their teams. Even in marriages, people are often more concerned with what they can get instead of what they can give.

It's not surprising that many twenty-first-century people are afraid. With as much relational pain as they endure, especially those who have served in ministry and leadership roles, it's no wonder they're gun shy. Amy and I talk often about our ministry scars. We've lost some of our closest friends to misunderstandings and false accusations. Doing what we believed was the right thing, we've had to fire people we cared about. Some still hate us to this day. Good friends have left the church bitter at us, or God, or both. People we opened up to betrayed confidences, dragging us through awkward seasons of pain and fear. For a while, we didn't ever want to trust again.

Maybe you can relate. Perhaps there was a time when you opened up to someone about your personal hurt only to have them belittle your pain. Or you trusted someone who ended up betraying you. Or you gave your heart to someone who walked away and rejected you. Unconsciously, you decided you'd make it on your own. You'd be independent, not needing anyone. Like Simon and Garfunkel, you might sing the classic folk song, "I have no need of friendship; friendship causes pain. It's laughter and it's loving I disdain. I am a rock. I am an island."

I can't tell you how many ministers I've talked to who are terrified to open up. They're paralyzed with fear, certain that if they let someone in, they'll get hurt — again. Maybe that's you. After being burned, now you live like so many others as a rock or an island. You're independent but acutely aware that something isn't quite right. You might have a constant low-grade frustration. Maybe you're plagued with a nagging sense of melancholy. You live in a persistent state of mild depression. You know something is missing, but you can't put your finger on what it is.

As long as you're afraid of intimacy and spiritual partnership, you won't likely experience *it*. To have *it*, you have to share *it* with each other. Just as there's no *I* in *team*, there's no *it* in *independence*.

When *it* walks alone, vultures circle and obituaries are written.

God told Adam that it isn't good to be alone. Solomon said that two are better than one. Jesus even said that God is present when two or three gather in his name. Those who have *it* experience it best together.

Ephesians 2:19 – 21 says, "You are citizens along with all of God's holy people. You are members of *God's family*. We are his house, built on the foundation of the apostles and the prophets. And the cornerstone is Christ Jesus himself. We who believe are carefully *joined together*, becoming a holy temple for the Lord" (NLT, emphasis mine). God wants you to be active members of his family. You are to be joined together. Henry Ford said, "Coming together is a beginning. Keeping it together is progress. Working together is success."[8]

You can't experience *it* alone. God wants you to share *it*. And yet for so many, the goal is to be independent. These well-intentioned people fail to realize that *to be independent is to be distinctly non-Christian.*

Did you get that? Many people pursue a goal that is opposed to God's plan. God designed you to be *interdependent.* He wants you depending on him *and* on his people. If you want *it*, you'll experience *it* best when you live in authentic community with God's people.

Blame the AC and the Garage-Door Opener

Where has the intimacy gone? Why are so many people relationally isolated? Why are people today living mostly independently and often alone? Blame it on the air conditioner and the garage-door opener! That's right. Before the air conditioner, people sat outside on their front porches and got to know one another. They sipped cool drinks, played checkers, and chatted for hours, sharing their lives. They had a healthy, laid-back togetherness. Then one day the air conditioner enabled people to stay indoors. In the absence of front-porch connections, neighbors started to drift. Relationships withered.

Enter the invention of the garage-door opener. Suddenly we could completely avoid the neighbors. (I told my kids that people used to have to get out of their cars to open the garage doors. They stared in disbelief.) Many new neighborhoods have no sidewalks, further discouraging interaction. Instead of having deep and lasting friendships with neighbors, many people hardly even know their neighbors' names.

What's more, technology has relieved us of the need to talk face to face. We can text or email instead, avoiding unpleasant topics and saving the time that deep conversations require. We can bank online, buy shoes online, do all of our Christmas shopping online, use self-service checkout lines, and never have to talk to anyone. We might be dependent on technology, but we no longer seem to be dependent on people.

Have you recognized this independent mindset bleeding into the church? Many people want to come to church services anony-

mously. Staff members want to work independently of the team. Yet the New Testament is peppered with "one another" reminders. While Scripture says to love one another, encourage one another, offer hospitality to one another, be kind to one another, many people are content tolerating one another, if not ignoring one another. My electronic Bible search program fails to find those one-anothers anywhere in the Bible!

Bringing *It* to Your Team

Some ministry teams have *it*. Some don't. The *it*-free or *it*-lite might be called a team, but they are really a group of individuals doing their own thing. A typical church might have a group that thinks about kids' ministry and another that focuses on drama and another that plans for missions. These groups are compartmentalized in nonporous silos. They're most passionate about what they're doing, forgetting how their role should fit into the overall mission of the church. Even if all the players are spiritual stars, the team will never win unless the players work together. Like Babe Ruth said, "The way a team plays as a whole determines its success. You may have the greatest bunch of individual stars in the world, but if they don't play together, the club won't be worth a dime."[9]

The apostle Paul used the body as a metaphor in 1 Corinthians 12:12: "The body is a unit, though it is made up of many parts; and though all its parts are many, they form one body." We each have our role. One person's role is to be the mouthpiece — communicating the vision. Another has the role of the hands — executing the work daily. Another fulfills the role of the feet — carrying the work and ministry outward. Yet another lives out the role of the spleen — okay, I have no idea what a spleen does, but you get the point.

The body needs all of the parts functioning together. A mouth or hand or foot or spleen lying on the ground by itself is not an "independent body part" — it's pointless. It's gross! Outside of the body, seeking to function on its own, a body part will cease to function. And it's the same in the church. That's why the independent ministry mindset kills *it*. Because *it* needs others with *it* to flourish.

No Ministry Is an Island

You might be familiar with the inner workings of staff members' competing for a limited number of resources. (I'm not talking about *your* church, of course.) A church's ministries quietly, or loudly, compete for budget dollars. They argue over who gets the use of certain rooms at certain times. Ministries compete for permission to hire administrative help. During building projects, each department might fight for their "fair share." Team leaders compete for accolades. *Will they mention me at the staff meeting?* And people might compete for the ministry leaders' time.

The problem is that when two parties compete, one loses. That's why in ministry, those who have *it* don't compete with one another; they work to *complete* one another. They love the mission so much they're willing to give and take. They're eager to work hard and play hard. They enjoy the battle. When they win, they win as a team. When they lose, they learn as a team. Someone said, "Teamwork is the fuel that allows common people to attain uncommon results."

Let's examine five common elements that contribute to *it* on the team.

1. Understanding the Big Picture

To be a strong team with *it*, every staff member and volunteer must understand the mission of the organization. This is where vision and camaraderie overlap and enhance each other. If a staff member doesn't see how her role fits into the big picture, she will wake up and feel like she is just doing a job. She'll feel undervalued, unappreciated, and unimportant. Her purpose must be expressed explicitly, not just assumed. Everyone needs his or her deserved share of the credit.

Imagine assembling a ten-thousand-piece puzzle. (My wife is smiling as she reads this. I feel nauseated. *I hate* puzzles.) If your role is to put ten pieces together in the corner, but you have no idea what difference your part makes, you'll quickly grow bored or frustrated. You'll want to know what you're contributing to. What will the completed puzzle look like? It's the leader's role to constantly point to the target, to express over and over how each person's role contributes. The big picture requires constant exposition.

When a person understands and embraces the mission, they'll enjoy and appreciate the camaraderie of sacrificing together. They willingly "give up" some things they love for something they love even more — reaching people for Christ. Mother Teresa said, "None of us, including me, ever do great things. But we can all do small things, with great love, and together we can do something wonderful."[10] Without regular reminders of why we do what we do, of how our part contributes to something wonderful, a team will lose *it* and simply be a bunch of people doing their own gig.

We once did an exercise that we called Because of You. We simply asked staff members to encourage each other by expressing how their role contributed to the larger work of God in the church. The conversation started with touching tones. Someone from our finance team told one of the kids' team members, "Because you write such great curriculum, my child is closer to Christ." Another person shared with someone on the facilities team, "Because you oversee the setup of chairs, God touches lives each week during worship." Before long, people were crying gently. One person openly sobbed as she expressed with heartfelt emotion, "Because of all of your encouragement and prayers, not only did my marriage survive, but we're closer than we ever could have imagined." Don't expect transparency and vulnerability to just happen; create opportunities for your team to bond. And when they can bond over the mission, in a way that helps them to see the big picture, well, that's just magic.

2. Having Fun Together

Those teams that have *it* enjoy *it* and enjoy each other. They laugh together, often. When I walk into the midst of an *it*-filled team in our church, I'm always wary of danger. At any moment, a rubber band could blindside me, a water gun could blast me, or someone could jump out from behind a desk and tackle me. I've been tackled on many occasions. Even full-on blitzed.

Teams with *it* have nicknames for everyone. (In case you're wondering, I'm Maverick and my video guy is Ice Man. Can you hear the theme song from the movie *Top Gun*?) They celebrate birthdays. They play gags on one another. They go to movies together. They take trips together. They tell stories about each other and exaggerate more with each telling. They initiate new members of the team. Those with *it* enjoy it together.

Speaking of initiations, when we hired Jerry Hurley, one of our key staff members, he listed his home for sale. To "welcome" him, another staff member and I made an appointment to meet his realtor for a showing at his house. The other staff member distracted the realtor while I unscrewed the lightbulbs, removed all the toilet paper, put cellophane over the toilets, and peeled all the labels off all the canned goods. When Jerry and his wife, Annette, returned, they thought the electricity was turned off, so Annette used the bathroom in the dark. Not seeing the cellophane, she made a mess all over herself and had no toilet paper to clean up with. (Pretty bad, I know. I cried when I heard about it. Really.) To top it all off, for the next few weeks they had a mystery vegetable every night with dinner.

All great teams provide this type of heartfelt, edifying ministry to each other.

Recently I met with Clay Baker, a friend who manages several hundred employees for a phone book company. He explained how his team was losing the

WHAT WHAT CONTRIBUTES TO **it**?

camaraderie of the past. He asked his leaders to reinstate some fun. When they proposed expensive and extravagant outings, he reminded them, "The best kind of fun is free." How true. Those with *it* don't have to pay for fun; they just have it.

3. Getting Naked Together

You may have read this subhead and thought, *Now that would be fun.* Or if you're more the stuffy religious type, you thought, *How disgusting.* Either way, it got your attention, didn't it?

Teams with great camaraderie get *relationally* naked. They take seriously the *it* in *nudity.* Those without *it* can be two-faced. Those with *it* are true-faced. There is no substitute for being transparent and real. The more real we are, the more likely we'll experience *it.* The more we hold back, the less likely we are to have it. Mark Sanborn, bestselling author and authority on leadership, says, "In teamwork, silence isn't golden; it's deadly."[11]

I refer to those I'm close to as my barefoot buddies. Amy says I have the ugliest feet in the world. If someone knocks on our door and we don't know who it is, she never says, "Craig, quick, get a shirt on." Topless Craig? No problem. What she always screams is, "Craig, quick, put some socks on. We can't let anyone see your feet!"

My intimate friends can see my feet. (If, of course, they can stomach it. It's a kind of training for *Fear Factor.*) They're my barefoot buddies. What's more, the women can show up without makeup. And the guys don't have to shave. And we can burp. We can bring our real selves.

You get the picture. We're open with each other. We bring our real selves. If one is hurting, the others know. We're family.

It is late Sunday evening as I'm typing in my office. Some of our closest friends just left our home. Amy and I are exhausted from this season of grueling (yet rewarding) ministry. Instead of sucking it up and striving to appear strong, we let it out and revealed our needs. Our close friends listened intently, then prayed for us passionately. We can already feel God lightening the burden.

Too many in ministry don't feel the liberty to show their real selves. Perhaps without realizing it, they're putting on a spiritual show, acting out a part really, all the while suffocating, dying a slow and lonely relational death.

Sydney Jourard writes about the benefits of self-disclosure. He describes it as "a function of attraction and trust." We become fond of someone who opens us to ourselves. He explains, "When people show that they like and trust us enough to share personal information, we begin to like and trust them in return. An expression of our new feeling, we are likely to disclose something about ourselves, thus strengthening the positive feelings."[12] That's why closed people rarely make friends. Mark it down: The more open your team is, the more likely you'll experience *it* together. The more closed you are, the more you'll kill *it*.

Our staff recently did 360 reviews. This is when team members review each other. The review starts out anonymously to encourage complete honesty. As the process continues, we get specific with each other to help one another bond and grow. Here are a few things team members said about me:

> "Craig is a great communicator and a visionary leader."

> "The most impactful aspect of Craig's leadership is his radically growing love for Jesus. His ability to transfer what God is doing in him is changing us as an organization."

> "Craig's disconnection with the day-to-day operations can be dangerous. His strength of delegating can become a weakness when he doesn't know what is going on."

> "Craig needs to be more engaged with staff members outside his immediate group. He would be surprised at what happens outside of his ministry values."

I was blessed and affirmed by the positive statements. And I was shaken that some consider me too disengaged. Imagine if

WHAT CONTRIBUTES TO it?

I didn't provide an opportunity to receive this kind of valuable information. I'd coast along assuming everything was on track without realizing that *it* had sprung a leak.

4. Celebrating the Wins

Many ministries have victories. Few celebrate them. A win is when something goes great. We pray. We plan. We perform. And God blesses it. But then we miss *it*, because we skip a critical step. We don't party.

Too many wins go by without celebrations.

I love what Andy Stanley does with his team at every staff meeting. They open their meetings with stories of how lives have been changed. They celebrate the victories, large and small. Everyone gets to enjoy what God has done, expressing together an attitude of gratitude.

Earlier in the day, I received an email from our youth team leader. One of our campuses had an extraordinary event during which God blew our socks off. (I wasn't there at the moment, which was fortunate because my feet ... well, you know.) The team leader included our whole staff in the email so we could celebrate the win. Later when I saw him approaching the building, I tackled him and threw him in the mud to celebrate. All day long he bragged about why his shirt was muddy. He was covered in *it* and he loved it ... celebrity for a day.

Teams with *it* look for excuses to celebrate. Anniversaries. Completion of significant projects. Ministry launches. Personal victories. This week, our finance team dressed up in eighties apparel to celebrate something. (I don't know what; I was afraid to ask.) The creative team brings in food regularly to celebrate birthdays and births of babies. I spend a lot of time testing the food just to make sure it's safe to eat. Don't underestimate the value of helping your whole church enjoy the wins. (My family's grocery bill is down $75 a month.)

Oprah Winfrey said, "The more you praise and celebrate your life, the more in life there is to celebrate."[13] Those with *it* celebrate *it* together.

5. Fighting Hard behind Closed Doors

Teams that have *it* are like family. And part of being family is fighting. That's right. Teams that have *it* know how to mix it up good and still be friends. They maintain their identity as a team, loyal to the end.

Pat Riley, coach of the Miami Heat, summarized loyalty to the team well when he said, "Commitment to the team — there is no such thing as in-between. You are either in or out."[14] Those with *it* are in. The opposite is true for the *it*-less. On the surface, they may look calm. But underneath, you'll often find a storm forming. People are nice and polite outwardly, but inwardly they are full of resentment and bitterness.

Part of having *it* is knowing that as a group we can have it out and still be friends. Any successful organization knows how to work through conflict. Teams without *it* avoid conflict. Teams with *it* understand that conflict is generally necessary to have *it*.

When a church has *it*, things move quickly. Change is constant. If you blink, you've missed something. Because of the rapid pace of progress, people can feel left out, uninformed, or unappreciated. Other times, opinionated people have very different ideas of what should happen. Sometimes these differences can be solved easily and quietly. Other times it takes a good old-fashioned fight to work things out.

Those with *it* know how to fight. When I talk about church fights, I don't mean the kind in which a deacon gets mad at the pastor and punches him at the deacons meeting, then the pastor's wife gets mad at the deacon's wife and crawls over and grabs her hair and claws her face while all the husbands cheer like they're watching Ultimate Fighting (and someone in the back is chanting, "Jer-*ry*! Jer-*ry*! Jer-*ry*!"). Those are definitely interesting fights, but

WHAT CONTRIBUTES TO it?

they're not productive. When I talk about a fight, I'm referring to shutting the doors and fighting fair in private. People with *it* know how to say what's on their minds, get it out in the open, and not walk out of the room until the issue is settled. Once it's resolved, they act publicly as if the fight never even happened.

Colin Powell said, "When we are debating an issue, loyalty means giving me your honest opinion, whether you think I'll like it or not. Disagreement, at this stage, stimulates me. But once a decision has been made, the debate ends. From that point on, loyalty means executing the decision as if it were your own."[15] Leaders with *it* fight together privately and stand together publicly. The functional word in both settings is *together*.

I work directly with four other directional leaders in the church. We have actually named our fights and laugh about them. There was the Blindside Craig Fight in which I almost fired them all. And there was the Naked by the Fire Pit Fight in which they almost fired me. (For the record, there was a fire pit, but no one was naked. Or someone really would have been fired.)

They Had *It* in Jerusalem

As a pastor of a large church, it's difficult to go anywhere locally without someone wanting to talk. A friend suggested that if I'm in a hurry, I can just put my cell phone up to my ear and pretend I'm talking. One day, while walking through Target, I gave his suggestion a try. I noticed how a few people politely waved, but no one stopped me. My new plan worked brilliantly until right in the middle of my "conversation." My cell phone rang. It was really loud.

Busted.

Instead of avoiding relationships and striving for independence, I'm asking God to make me *inter*dependent, like the believers of the early church. Remember when Peter preached in Jerusalem on the day of Pentecost and three thousand people met Christ? These new believers had *it* in a special way. Without Starbucks coffee in the lobby, without four-color mailers, and without an awesome website to rely on, these believers depended on God's presence and his people. They had *it*, and it spread rapidly. Scripture shows:

- The believers were devoted to God's Word, to spending time together, and to each other (Acts 2:42).
- Because of their commitment, everyone was blown away by what God was doing (Acts 2:43).
- They were so committed to each other that if someone had a need, someone else would sell something and give the money to them. They were so generous that eventually no one had a need (Acts 2:44 – 45; 4:34).
- They spent time together in their homes. They had refrigerator rights (Acts 2:46).
- God gave them great favor with people, who begged to be a part. Others saw *it* and wanted *it*. People were being saved every day (Acts 2:47).

Where is that Acts 2 kind of community today? Instead of giving our lives to each other deeply and depending on one another, many are avoiding each other. The guy at the gym with his iPod, signaling to everyone, "Leave me alone." The person who spends limitless screen-to-screen time with people, but virtually no face-to-face time. People are doing life alone.

Someone said, "Teamwork is the fuel that allows common people to attain uncommon results." In the next chapter, we'll see how this camaraderie, partnership, teamwork, and family, fueled with passion from God, can overcome almost any obstacle by contributing to another *It* Factor — innovative thinking.

- The people on teams that have *it* enjoy *it* together.
- As long as you're afraid of intimacy and spiritual partnership, you likely won't experience *it*.
- To have *it*, you have to share *it* with each other. *It* dies when it is alone.
- Leaders with *it* understand the big picture, have fun, get naked, celebrate the wins, and fight behind closed doors.

 FACTORS

Questions for Discussion or Reflection

1 Many people are striving for independence rather than learning to be interdependent. How are the people in your ministry growing together and becoming more dependent on God and others? How are those around you isolating themselves and becoming more independent? What needs to be done to make improvements?

2 Teams that have *it* enjoy *it* together. They have a blast with each other. How is your organization fostering great team spirit? What are you doing in your everyday interactions that everyone enjoys? What are your plans to develop camaraderie?

3 How well do your team members know one another? Would people describe your organization as a caring environment? How many of your team members have refrigerator rights at your house? What could you do to invite more people into your life and the heart of the team? Do you have a best friend at work? How would your other team members respond to that question?

4 How well do your team members understand the big picture? Do people know the value of their role and see how it fits in the grand scheme? Or do they feel like they're just doing a job? Are your team members competing for resources or completing each other? Explain. What can you do to better paint the vision and show value to those serving?

WHAT CONTRIBUTES TO **it?**

Perry Noble
NewSpring Church
Anderson, South Carolina

> *When a team feels like a family, they will go all out to love and serve one another.*
>
> —PERRY NOBLE

In 1999, Perry Noble selected a small core group from within a college Bible study to become the beginning of NewSpring Church. This small group of committed believers prayed passionately for the people of Anderson, South Carolina, a community with nearly 48 percent of the population classified as unchurched.

On January 16, 2000, 115 people attended NewSpring's first Sunday morning service at Anderson College. By 2002, NewSpring had moved to the largest auditorium on campus and was holding four weekly services averaging 3,500 people in attendance. In January 2006, NewSpring finished construction on its very own, state-of-the-art facility complete with a 2,500-seat auditorium and kids' space. As of today, more than 8,000 people worship weekly at NewSpring, with hundreds meeting Christ as Lord.

Among many things, the staff at NewSpring is known for having a blast together. This relational passion isn't accidental. It is a direct reflection of some of Perry's core beliefs about friendship and teamwork. Quoting John Maxwell, Perry says that "teamwork makes the dream work." God's work at NewSpring is proof.

I asked Perry to give me a behind-the-scenes glimpse at how he created this environment of camaraderie. Perry explained, "Reality is this — there are many days that I will spend way more waking hours with the people at my office than with my wife and child. I've *got* to know that we are a team. As a leader I cannot ever feel like someone hasn't fully bought it — that's just not good for my mental health and the health of the organization."

Perry offers the obvious reminder that life happens to people — even staff members at churches. Kids get sick. Parents pass away. People battle health challenges. And in many churches across the world, no one ministers to the ministers. That's why Perry passionately exclaims, "If the staff has a sense of family, they will support and take care of one another — which makes the entire organization a better place to work."

To develop a fun and caring environment, the NewSpring staff does several things:

- The senior management team takes two annual trips. The staff will pray and plan, but a major part of the trip is devoted to goofing off and bonding. Once, a group went bungee jumping together.
- The staff regularly shuts down the office to do a fun activity like bowling or playing putt-putt.
- At the staff meetings, new staff members have to share random facts about themselves. Occasionally they've performed songs or dances for the rest of the team.
- Perry invites the whole staff into fun yet revealing conversations. He might ask everyone to share about their first date or to talk honestly about what God is doing in their lives.
- The work environment is focused and yet incredibly fun. It is not uncommon to see Perry or others playing games, tossing a ball, or playing practical jokes.

If a church staff has grown relationally flat, Perry advises that team to address the challenge head on. If there are issues below the surface (and there probably are), Perry says the team members "must be willing to say anything behind closed doors." He advises a "do whatever it takes" philosophy to get things out in the open and resolve any challenges.

If a ministry staff grows dull, the creativity and spark can fade. Perry stresses that a fun environment is a reflection of intentional randomness and unpredictability. Perry challenges leaders to plan to do something fun, then just do it. Don't expect it to just happen. Make it happen. Perry says, "Teams do not have to grow flat, but they will over time if the leader doesn't make an effort to keep things fun."

NewSpring also stresses that they would never hire someone they don't like. Perry says laughingly, "Life is too short to spend forty to fifty hours around people who do nothing but stress you out and make you desire to go and stick your head in a blender. I really do love the guys I serve with. They are my best friends. I love their families. I love their walk with God. I love the fact that they actually think I know what I'm doing. And if there is ever a relational rift between us, I address it, and I challenge them always to do the same. We cannot be effective if we don't like one another."

SEVEN

INNOVATIVE MINDS:

YOU'LL DO ANYTHING FOR it

Innovation is not absolutely necessary, but then neither is survival.

—*Andrew Papageorge*

Imagine if I asked you, "Could you come up with a hundred thousand dollars in cash by the end of this week?" Chances are unless you're megarich, you'd probably say, "Wutchu talkin' 'bout, Willis?" In your mind, I just asked you to do the impossible. You might think, *There's no way I could come up with that kind of cash.*

I can barely pay my bills. If that's your first reaction, you'd be like most people.

Now let's do another imaginary exercise. Think about the people you love most in the world. Your short list might include your spouse, your parents, your kids, and some very close, trusted friends. Think of one of those people specifically. (I'm thinking about my four-year-old Bookie because he just ran by smiling and shouted, "Daddy, isn't this a funderful day?") Do you have your person in mind? Good. Let's keep going.

Suppose I told you that your special loved one is very sick. I'm not talking about the "I've got to go puke my guts up for an hour bowing reverently before the porcelain god" sick. I'm referring to the "you've got less than a month to live" sick. Certainly I'd have your undivided attention.

Now imagine my telling you that the doctors are certain that your loved one has no chance of living beyond the month unless you get them a very rare shot by the end of this week. And because of the scarcity of this shot, it is *very* expensive.

You're probably thinking, *Money is no object! If this shot will cure my loved one, I'll do whatever it takes!*

"How much is the shot?" you ask, determined to find the money.

Soberly, I reply, "The shot is one hundred thousand dollars."

What would you do?

Remember a couple of minutes ago you thought finding a hundred thousand dollars in a few days would be impossible. But now, your perspective has changed. Even though it will be difficult, you'll find a way to get the money. You might secure a home equity loan. You might call a rich relative. You might sell everything you own. You might even consider knocking off a bank. (I hope not, but you just might find yourself keeping your ski mask handy.) Why are you now willing to go to such extremes? Because you just became motivated.

What changed? In the first scenario I gave you no incentive. But the life-and-death stakes in the second scenario made you unstoppable.

The spark of passion ignited the fuel for innovation.

WHAT CONTRIBUTES TO **it?**

One Idea Could Change Everything

Wikipedia defines innovation as the process of making improvements by introducing something new. If there is any group in the world that should be motivated to make improvements, reflecting God's creative nature, it should be Christians. *Imago Dei* is the Latin term expressing the idea that human beings are created in the image of God. Since we're made in the image of a creative creator, we too can conceive creative ideas. Psychologist, physician, and consultant Edward de Bono said, "There is no doubt that creativity is the most important human resource of all. Without creativity, there would be no progress, and we would be forever repeating the same patterns."[16]

Reflecting God, innovative believers tend to have *it*. And *it* is borne out of their passion to please God, reach people, and help those in need. At our church, we encourage people to do anything short of sin to reach those who don't know Christ. With increasing passion comes increasing creativity to reach people.

The apostle Paul obviously had *it*. And he often did things in new ways. He crossed lines and changed his approach to reach different people. He said, "To the Jews I became like a Jew, to win the Jews.... To the weak I became weak, to win the weak. I have become all things to all men so that by all possible means I might save some" (1 Cor. 9:20, 22).

With-*it* ministries are filled with people so passionate, they're driven to become innovative. They'll become like others or do unusual things to reach those who are far from Christ or to help those who are hurting. Like the four men who broke through the roof to get their crippled friend to Jesus, motivated believers don't see obstacles. They create opportunities.

Instead of saying, "It will never work," they say, "What if this does work?"

Instead of whining, "We can't reach certain people," with faith they exclaim, "We will find a way."

While many lament, "We don't have what it takes to make a difference," innovative leaders say, "God is our provider; we have more than enough."

These innovators reflect Robert Schuller's heart when he said, "All it takes is one idea to solve an impossible problem."[17] They commit to find that idea — and usually succeed.

Embrace Your Limitations

In 2006 and 2007, our church was named the most innovative church in America and was featured in *Outreach* magazine. I was honored, yet openly acknowledged that it's the people around me who are the innovative ones. I'm just the guy crazy enough to let them try their whacked-out ideas. (For the record, I believe the most innovative leaders are the ones most of us haven't heard of yet.)

Because of this honor, I've sometimes been invited to consult and to speak on the topic of innovation. Before I speak on the subject, the two most common complaints I hear from leaders are:

1. We just don't have any creative people.
2. If only we had more money, we could be really creative.

While I acknowledge that an abundance of resources opens many possibilities, I'd argue that these two complaints are simply excuses that prevent many great ideas from becoming a reality. In fact, our leaders have stumbled upon something that's changed the

WHAT CONTRIBUTES TO it?

way we do ministry. Maybe you've heard the old adage, "Where God guides, he always provides." We made up a new saying: "God often guides by what he doesn't provide."

Read that again slowly and think about it in relation to your ministry. God often guides by what he *doesn't* provide. Are you up against a wall with no good plan to get past it? Have you hit an obstacle that appears impenetrable? Maybe God will guide you to see something that you couldn't have seen if he'd just removed the wall.

One of the greatest examples of this principle is found in Acts 3. Peter and John were traveling to their afternoon temple prayer meeting when they saw a man, who'd been crippled his whole life, being carried to his begging post. The hurting beggar recognized Peter and held out his cup, hoping to get some change to buy dinner. That's when God started using Peter's limitations — what Peter didn't have — to guide him. Think about it. If Peter had had a few bucks on him, it might've been easy to toss a bill toward the man, nod politely, and keep moving to be on time for prayer. But because he didn't have what the man *wanted*, he was able to give the man what he *needed*. Peter said, "Silver or gold *I do not have*, but what I have I give you. In the name of Jesus Christ of Nazareth, walk" (Acts 3:6, emphasis mine). Then Peter reached down and pulled the man to his feet. I wonder if this would have happened if Peter hadn't been financially limited.

The truth: you have what you need. Watch out for the excuses. Most of us make them occasionally. Maybe you've thought:

- We could do so much more if only our people gave more.
- We could reach more people if we had a better building.
- We could have an awesome ministry if we could afford more staff.

Whenever you're tempted to whine about what you don't have, remember that God has given you everything you need to do everything he wants you to do. Second Peter 1:3 says, "Everything that goes into a life of pleasing God has been miraculously given to us by getting to know, personally and intimately, the One who invited us to God" (MSG). If you don't have something you *think* you need, maybe it's because God wants you to see something you've never seen. Those with *it* recognize that God brings *it*. *It* is not found in the things the eye can see.

The Limitation Can Drive the Innovation

We've raised two critical *It* Factors of great innovation:

1. *Passion* creates motivation, which leads to innovation. You couldn't come up with a hundred thousand dollars in a few days unless you had a great reason to do it. Then you'd find a way.
2. *Limitations* often reveal opportunities. They help you to see things that you might have otherwise missed.

Put these factors together and you get:

Limited Resources + Increasing Passion = Exponential Innovation

Your greatest ministry innovation could come from your greatest limitation — *if* you have a sincere passion to reach and care for people. When you ask God for eyes to see, you may see what has always been there but you've never noticed before. Have you ever bought a car, and then as you drove it around the first week noticed dozens of other people driving the same car? They were all around you last week; you just didn't have the mindset to see them. Limitations and passion have a way of changing our minds and our eyes.

God did this for us at LifeChurch.tv. When our church was several years old, we built our first building with an auditorium that could seat about six hundred people. Within a year, it was full four times over. In our limited thinking, we'd run into a wall. Adding more services seemed impossible. We knew we couldn't financially afford to build again. Even if we could, it would take way too long. With nowhere to grow, we were afraid we might lose *it*.

That's when God gave us a shot of creativity. Thankfully, our team consists of passionate leaders who asked God to transform this obstacle into an opportunity. After praying and brainstorming, someone suggested we consider meeting at a second location. To our knowledge, that had never been done before. (We were unaware that the practice was far from new and was being done around the world.)

Armed with passion, we approached a movie theater and asked if we could hold worship experiences there on Sundays. This is common practice today, but at the time, the theater had never considered such an option. They said yes, and overnight our greatest limitation became the catalyst for what we considered a great innovation: the multisite church.

When people started worshiping at the theater, they found *it*. They excitedly invited others to attend church in such a nontraditional environment. They gave guests every reason to come, explaining that you could eat popcorn in church, sit in comfortable chairs, and even make out in the back row!

God wasn't finished showing us new things. Shortly after adding this second meeting place, my wife gave birth to our fourth child of six, Sam. (Yes, I said six. I can't keep my wife off me. And yes, we know what causes babies. It's just one of those habits we're having a tough time breaking.) Sam was born at four a.m. on a Sunday morning. I knew that if I left my wife at the hospital so I could preach, it would be my last sermon and my kids would grow up as orphans. I'd be dead and my wife would be in jail for murder. I panicked. *What are we going to do? We can't get a staff member ready to teach this fast. We can't find a guest preacher at four a.m.* With no other options, we decided to run the video of the message from Saturday night.

And it worked! Why? Because *it* worked! Another obstacle, another innovation: the video message. Those small ideas have enabled us to reach thousands and thousands of people we might not have reached otherwise. If you're facing an obstacle right now, maybe God will increase your passion and give you a breakthrough idea. And your breakthrough idea might help give your ministry more *it* than ever before.

Leadership guru Peter Drucker said, "An established company which, in an age demanding innovation, is not able to innovate, is doomed to decline and extinction."[18] Though he was referring to businesses, I'd argue this quote applies to churches as well. What obstacle are you facing? Ask God for breakthrough thinking. Don't think about small changes. Think radically. Think out of the box. Destroy the box! Roger Enrico, former chairman of Pepsico, said, "Beware of the tyranny of making small changes to small things. Rather, make big changes to big things."[19] For the sake of those who don't know Christ, think big.

Break the Rules

Most of the greatest spiritual innovators throughout history were people who broke the rules. Thomas Edison said, "There ain't no rules here. We're trying to accomplish something."[20] People with *it* do life differently than people without *it*.

WHAT CONTRIBUTES TO *it*?

No one is a better example than Jesus. By the Pharisees' standards, Jesus failed daily, because they measured success by their own rules. He broke the Sabbath. He hung out with the wrong people. His disciples were uneducated. He did things upside down and backward.

And he fulfilled God's perfect will and paid the price for our sins. According to the Pharisees, Jesus failed. According to God, he became the savior of the world.

When you try something new in ministry, most people will tell you that your idea will never work. Leadership expert Warren Bennis said, "Innovation ... by definition will not be accepted at first. It takes repeated attempts, endless demonstrations, monotonous rehearsals before innovation can be accepted and internalized by an organization. This requires *courageous patience*."[21] If you have a God idea, you must be brave enough to go with it. Break some rules.

Martin Luther broke a big rule. When the church said the common person wasn't spiritually mature enough to handle the Word of God, Luther disagreed. He broke the rules by innovatively translating the Bible into German and putting it into the hands of the everyday person.

John Wesley broke some rules. It was considered heresy to preach outside of a church building. When he was kicked out of his church, he preached outdoors. His passion to preach Christ mixed with the limited availability of indoor venues drove him to invent the open-air meeting (which paved the way for the drive-in theater). This breakthrough opened doors for many others, such as Billy Graham.

Modern-day leaders, including Bill Hybels, Rick Warren, Mark Driscoll, Ed Young Jr., Andy Stanley, Erwin McManus, Brian Houston, David Yonggi Cho, T. D. Jakes, and others, broke the rules and led the church in new and innovative ways. Who knows how many people have come to Christ because creative leaders with *it* broke the rules?

Prepare to Offend

As God blesses your ministry with *it*, remember that those without *it* tend to criticize those with *it*, especially when you do things differently. Larry Ellison, billionaire CEO of the Oracle Corporation, said, "When you innovate, you've got to be prepared for everyone telling you you're nuts."[22]

Take, for example, the very first hot air balloon. "On June 4, 1783, at the market square of the French village of Annonay, not far from Paris, a smoky bonfire on a raised platform was fed by wet straw and old wool rags. Tethered above, straining its lines, was a huge taffeta bag thirty-three feet in diameter. In the presence of 'a respectable assembly and a great many other people,' and accompanied by great cheering, the balloon was cut from its moorings and set free to rise majestically into the noon sky. Six thousand feet into the air it went — the first public ascent of a balloon, the first step in the history of human flight. It came to earth several miles away in a field, where it was promptly attacked by pitchfork-waving peasants and torn to pieces as an instrument of evil!"[23]

Jesus experienced resistance to the irregular almost daily. When he healed a woman who'd been crippled by a spirit for eighteen years, the Pharisees were offended because he did it on the Sabbath. According to Matthew 12, Jesus' healing on the Sabbath motivated the Pharisees to scheme to kill him. That is *funny*. You can't heal on the Sabbath but you can plot murder! Get ready to offend some Pharisees.

What's accepted today was often rejected at first. In 1876, Western Union circulated an internal memo which read, "This 'telephone' has too many shortcomings to be seriously considered as a means of communication. The device is of no value to us."[24] Innovations in the Christian community are no exception. So much of what is accepted today was despised just a few years ago. For example, people screamed "heresy" when Martin Luther used the printing press to make the Bible available to the public. Generally accepted practices today, which would have been condemned in many churches just a few decades ago, include dressing casually for church, clapping during worship, and presenting dramas in church. The innovation of multisite churches and video teaching is still despised and rejected by many. I'm guessing they will be generally accepted in less than five years.

WHAT CONTRIBUTES TO it?

Yesterday's controversy can become today's norm. And today's contemporary becomes tomorrow's traditional. When you have *it*, you'll find new ways to spread *it*. But be prepared for what goes with *it* — criticism.

Besides the usual list of criticisms of multisite churches, video teaching, and megachurches, here is the short list of what we've been criticized for in the last year:

- Creating a campus in Second Life (the online virtual world).
- Giving our ministry material away.
- Creating www.youversion.com to foster an online Bible community.
- Partnering with other churches to create new campuses.
- Producing a video promotion for my book *Going All the Way*, called "Don't Pet the Squirrel."
- Experimenting with video worship.
- Putting up billboards that said, "Satan hates LifeChurch.tv" and pointing people to the website www.satanhateslife.com.
- Even though Amy and I consider ourselves environmentally responsible, we've been criticized for driving a Suburban. (We just couldn't fit all eight of us in a Honda Accord.)

Don't let the rules of man stop you from following God. When he gives *it* to you, go with *it*.

Too Much of a Good Thing Can Kill *It*

When you have *it*, you might get on a roll with new and innovative ideas. But be careful; too much of a good thing can kill *it*.

I worked with the leaders of a great church that unquestionably had *it* for years. During the early days of the church, the people were passionate, generous, committed, and growing spiritually. They brought their friends. Hundreds were saved. They had an impact on the community.

Over time, they built several buildings: phases one, two, and three. As the church grew, instead of using volunteers to lead worship, they hired pros. Rather than enlisting members to stack chairs after church each week, they paid a staff. Instead of preaching passionate and raw messages, the pastor enlisted a research team and used other methods that kept the teaching at arm's length.

Outwardly they were improved; inwardly they developed an immunity to the fever that once had driven them. The weekend experiences used to be rougher around the edges. Now they were professionally produced with dress rehearsals and detailed tech and sound checks. Even with all these "better" tools, the church lost something. They appeared slick, produced, and lacking what had made them special before. Their *it* had quit.

Kathy Sierra, in her Creating Passionate Users blog, asks, "What makes indie films more appealing than so many of the huge Hollywood productions? What makes indie music more interesting than the slick big-label, big-production records? What's the magic that disappears when you hear the studio-mix version of something you once heard live? Not that most of us have the problem of too big a budget for our own good, but still … maybe we should think about whether some imperfections might be a *good* thing. Maybe we should consider whether we're trying too hard to smooth all the rough edges."

Then she offers what she calls the Imperfections Curve.

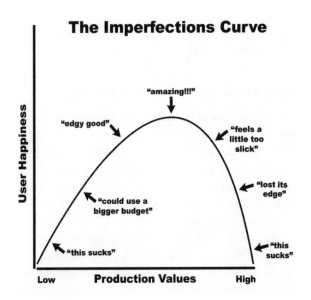

The Imperfections Curve

User Happiness

"amazing!!!"

"edgy good"

"feels a little too slick"

"lost its edge"

"could use a bigger budget"

"this sucks"

"this sucks"

Low   **Production Values**   High

WHAT CONTRIBUTES TO **it?**

Those with *it* grow even more passionate about reaching people. But don't get tricked into trusting your spiritual bells and whistles or you might become too slick, lose your edge, then lose *it*. God doesn't need what many churches think are necessities to reach people. Don't put your faith in the innovations. Keep your faith in Christ.

Tell the Devil to Go to Hell

Tom Kelley starts his book *The Ten Faces of Innovation* with this paragraph: "We've all been there. The pivotal meeting where you push forward a new idea or proposal you're passionate about. A fast-paced discussion leads to an upwelling of support that seems to reach critical mass. And then, in one disastrous moment, your hopes are dashed when someone weighs in with those fatal words: 'Let me just play the Devil's Advocate for a minute ...' "[25] After making that seemingly harmless statement, the person feels free to blast your idea to smithereens.

Your new idea *will* face resistance. It may or may not work. In the next chapter, we'll talk about the necessity of failure on the road to success. Don't let the devil's advocate kill God's plan. Decide today that your team will work together to find new ways to reach people, not more reasons to stay the same. And when someone does try to take the devil's deadly role, tell the devil he can go to hell.

- God often guides by what he doesn't provide.
- Increasing Passion + Limited Resources = Exponential Innovation
- You have everything you need to do what God wants you to do.
- Innovative leaders do anything short of sin to reach the lost.
- "All it takes is one idea to solve an impossible problem" (Robert Schuller).

WHAT CONTRIBUTES TO **it?**

Questions for Discussion or Reflection

1 Many churches make excuses for not trying something new. Some believe they don't have creative people. Others claim they lack resources. Which of these excuses has affected your ministry? Remember you have everything you need to do what God wants you to do. What resources (people, buildings, technology) are underutilized? What is God showing you?

2 Is your ministry community one that encourages innovation? If so, what are the factors that drive ministry innovation? If not, what is stopping innovation? What can you do to change the culture and encourage creative forms of ministry?

3 Have you hit something in your ministry that appears to be an obstacle? For the next ten minutes, brainstorm solutions. No idea is a bad idea. During your brainstorming, don't let anyone say, "Yes, but ..." On every idea that comes up, force people to say, "Yes, and ..."

4 What idea has been simmering inside you? Is there something new God is calling you to do that may be hated for a while but changes lives for years to come? What are you going to do about it?

PROFILE

Tim Stevens
Granger Community Church
Granger, Indiana

> *Do what you do because Jesus is watching, not so you'll end up on some top 100 church list or be the envy of the next pastors gathering. That stuff doesn't matter. Be innovative because you believe people matter and you want to please Jesus.*
>
> —TIM STEVENS

Tim Stevens is the executive pastor of Granger Church. Granger ministers to more than 5,500 people each weekend in Granger, Indiana. This United Methodist Church is applauded nationwide as one of the most innovative churches in the country.

Innovative ministry seems to be second nature to this group of leaders. When I asked Tim what drives his church to be so creative, he answered, "The mission. We desperately want to reach people who are far from God and help them take steps toward Jesus. None of us are encumbered by tradition, so we'll do anything to reach them."

Tim shared some of the innovative ways they're doing church. First, he says that unlike many large churches, Granger is a team-based ministry. Although Mark Beeson is the lead pastor, he leads by empowering the team around him. Tim says, "We find great leaders and let them lead."

WHAT CONTRIBUTES TO it?

Granger is also well known for using highly creative and effective message series to engage people in the community. After deciding on a teaching topic, his team looks for cultural packaging to put around the topic that will make it easier to invite unchurched friends to church. For example, during a series on how to make a difference in life, they asked, "Is there a pop culture tie-in we can use to make it easy for people to invite their friends?" Granger chose the television show *Heroes*, which was launching a new season the same time as their new series.

Granger also recognizes that most people who meet Christ do so before they are eighteen years of age. Armed with this knowledge, the church leaders shine with innovative approaches to reaching kids using innovative buildings. Their team designed a children's facility that compels the kids to beg their parents to bring them to church. The rooms are interactive and designed for a specific age. After the kids check in on the main level, they get into a slide (like the ones at McDonald's playland) and zoom around and pop out in their class-room on the lower level.

The leaders are also designing innovative space for the adults. Granger recently planned a twenty thousand square-foot space that will be used to experience the service in the context of community (rather than in straight rows facing forward). People will be able to invite friends to join them in this informal space, which will have the live services piped in to plasma screens so that people can converse during the learning process. This space is intended to reach those who have a different learning style or aren't ready to take the big step into the auditorium.

If you ever worship at Granger Church, you'll experience a high-definition video wall that is fifty feet wide and twenty-five feet tall, along with four additional video screens. Tim explains that this emerged as a response to the media-driven culture. The church uses the backdrops for stunning visuals during the messages, music videos behind live songs, and other video elements throughout the service. The service is now designed with visuals on the screen for the entire sixty to sixty-five minute experience.

I asked Tim what he would say to encourage other pastors and leaders to become more innovative to reach people for Christ. He said:

- Everything you need to be innovative is already in your church. God has gifted people who attend your church whom you haven't even met yet. Creativity attracts creative people and innovation attracts innovative people.

- Do your ministry with excellence and push the envelope on creativity, and others in your church who are wired the same way will rise to the surface and help you take it even farther.
- Don't be afraid to try new things. But also don't be afraid to do something that's already been done. Just because you are copying something another church did doesn't mean it won't be effective in your town.

Tim offered a valuable reminder: "The goal isn't innovation. The goal is effectiveness. We strive for innovation because we want to be effective. Innovation can be confused with cool and hip and trendy. There's nothing wrong with cool or hip, but that may not be innovative at all. You might show up for church in suspenders and a cowboy hat in order to get people's attention and make a point, and it might be incredibly effective. Cool and hip? Definitely not. But it is innovative."

EIGHT

WILLINGNESS TO FALL SHORT:

YOU FAIL TOWARD it

> Only those who dare to fail greatly can ever achieve greatly.
>
> —*Robert F. Kennedy*

all six of my children are walking now. (And out of diapers. Thank God!) Truthfully, I miss watching my little ones progress from rolling over to sitting up to crawling to standing to finally venturing out with no visible means of support. When they take their first steps, their eyes always grow huge with a mixture of excitement and fear as they wobble like a two-foot-tall Frankenstein. No matter what — whether it's after the first step or the third — they always fall. Always.

Imagine if, immediately following their first tumble, one of them thought, *Well, that's that. I gave it a shot. Things didn't work out. I'm not meant to be a walker. I guess I'll just crawl the rest of my life.* The fear of failure causes many ministries to think with this same kind of absurdity. And on they crawl while God wants them to soar.

The *it*-ified ministries that I've observed fail *often*. They're led by aggressive, do-what-it-takes, thick-skinned people who are willing to make mistakes. They're not afraid to fail. In contrast, the ministries without *it* are usually the ones playing it safe, doing only what is sure to succeed. As counterintuitive as it sounds, failing often can help a ministry experience *it*. Being overly cautious can kill *it*.

On the surface, these ideas don't seem to make sense. But they're true. Aggressive leaders with *it* are often dreaming, experimenting, and testing the limits. They don't know what can't be done and are willing to try things others think aren't possible. Because of their conquering nature, these passionate spiritual entrepreneurs take risks and at first glance don't appear to succeed. They fail often. But when they do fail, they tend to rebound quickly. Temporary failures are often followed by lasting success. They try, fail, learn, adjust, and try again. After a series of accidental learning experiences, these hard-hitting leaders often stumble onto innovative ministry ideas they never would have discovered without rolling the dice. As John Dewey once said, "Failure is instructive. The person who really thinks, learns quite as much from his failures as from his successes."[26]

Failing Forward

The person in Scripture who best exemplifies the "fail often" principle is probably Peter. I relate to him because he had great intentions but often messed up in dramatic fashion. Even though he was far from perfect, Peter still had *it*. Perhaps what led Peter to *it*-land when others missed the on-ramp was his willingness to fail. If Peter were alive today, he would understand as well as anyone what Walter Brunell meant when he said, "Failure is the tuition you pay for success."

WHAT CONTRIBUTES TO it?

Think about how many times Peter's aggressive nature led to what we could call great "learning opportunities." He once offered unsolicited advice to Jesus, insisting that Jesus *not* give up his life. Jesus, the master teacher, rewarded Peter by calling him Satan. I'm guessing that got Peter's attention. I have many names I dream of Jesus calling me — friend, son, faithful servant — but Satan is not one of them.

Another time Peter hopped out of a boat (while the other eleven disciples played it safe) and walked on water toward Jesus before losing focus and faith, and sinking like a, well, *peter* (that's Greek for "rock"). Another great — and wet — lesson.

Then there was the time Peter loyally defended Jesus by swinging his sword at a temple guard's head, slightly missing the center of his target and instead clipping off the poor guy's ear. Again Jesus offered Peter more valuable instruction. And right after that, Peter failed the mother of all failures when he denied Jesus three times. The full impact of this lesson sunk in for Peter only after the resurrection, when Jesus forgave him and restored him to a position of huge responsibility — CEO of what would become God's worldwide marketing enterprise. That's not normally the way we reward failures, but God's different.

Peter's education consisted of trying, failing, learning, adjusting, and trying again. His "failing forward" most likely contributed to God's decision to choose Peter as the guest speaker on the day of Pentecost. Peter failed often. He learned from his failures. Then he led three thousand people to Christ and helped birth the church.

As a marketing major in college, I was trained to get people's attention. This asset became a curse when I unintentionally hurt some church leaders with a billboard campaign targeted at the unchurched. Our outreach strategy included billboards that read, "Think church is boring and outdated? So did we." Another one said, "Hate church? So did we." Each statement was followed by the line "LifeChurch.tv — not what you'd expect." Although these signs drew the attention of our target crowd, they also drew fire from an unintended group — other churches. In my heart, I wasn't taking shots at other churches. Yet other leaders took offense. When I put myself in their shoes, I understood why. I had to admit my

Love God, but hate church?

LIFECHURCH.TV
www.lifechurch.tv

So did we.

mistake and learn from it. Now I'm careful to build up other churches and strive never to make another ministry look bad.

Those who fail forward can relate to Michael Jordan, one of the greatest basketball players of all time, who said, "I've missed more than nine thousand shots in my career. I've lost almost three hundred games. Twenty-six times, I've been trusted to take the game-winning shot and missed. I've failed over and over and over again in my life. And that is why I succeed."[27]

Failing Past Your Local Max

Seth Godin writes in his blog, and also in his book *Small Is the New Big*, about the idea of a "local max." He explains that when an organization is struggling to move forward, its leaders are likely trying to understand the true nature of peak performance.

Godin explains, "Everyone starts at that dot at the bottom left corner. You're not succeeding because you haven't started yet. Then you try something. If it works, you end up at point A ... Of course, being a success-oriented capitalist, that's not enough. So you do more. You push and hone and optimize until you end up at the Local Max. [By "local max," Godin seems to mean the place of one's most comfortable success.] The Local Max is where your efforts really pay off. So you try harder. And you end up at point B. Point B is a bummer. Point B is backwards. Point B is where the outcome of more effort against your strategy doesn't return better results. So you retreat. You go back to your Local Max."[28]

In the church world, this is where most people stay. To move past the local max is risky. You'll likely make some mistakes, fail, and struggle. So most people stick with what they know. But according to Godin, the local max chart is incomplete. The chart really looks like this:

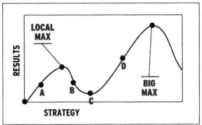

The difference between your local max and the big max may be one or two failures followed by seasons of learning. *It* is not that far away. The problem is you have to go through point C. Those who lack *it* are afraid of C. Disheartened by setbacks, they pull back and start avoiding risks. They slide back to their former place of mastery. They stop growing as leaders and freeze in time.

But *it*-owners push through the failures. They know that setbacks can be setups for better things to come. They study their failures and learn from them. When those with *it* fail, they try to fail forward.

Failure Is Not an Option

One church I've followed had *it* for years. This unique and special ministry was built by leaders who failed often. These brave spiritual pioneers rolled the dice, often seeming to lose their gambles. But with each failure, the entrepreneurial leaders learned, adjusted, and attacked again. They discovered new ways of doing ministry and set an example for churches around the world.

Then one day, this church realized they had accomplished a lot. They had churches across the world looking to them, following every move. Feeling the weight of being such a respected example, the leaders grew more and more cautious. Within a few years, these formerly most daring of Christian leaders played it safe.

I once met with a few of these greats, and I tossed out a few off-the-wall ideas. One of them explained to me, in a tone that almost seemed apologetic, "Craig, when you get to where we are, you can't afford to make mistakes. For us, failure is not an option."

My heart broke. These were my heroes, the ones who mortgaged their homes for the vision of the church. They had endured harsh criticism for their ministry experiments. Sometimes they succeeded. Often they failed. But they learned. They grew. They broke through ceilings. They busted barriers. They shattered paradigms. They led the way for thousands to follow. They had *it* like few other churches I'd known. And now they were starting to lose *it*.

This leader's quote is stuck in my mind: "Failure is not an option." I agree wholeheartedly. In our meetings I repeat it to our staff over and over again, with a little twist: "Failure is not an option. *It is essential.*"

The *it*-ish understand: failure is a part of success. Woody Allen said, "If you're not failing every now and again, it's a sure sign you're not trying anything very innovative."[29] Because great leaders are generally innovative, they're also often scared. They're betting the farm. They're swinging for the fence. Those who swing hard will strike out often. But they'll also knock some out of the park.

For the record, my friends at the church who decided they would never fail ... they're starting to fail again. And guess what? They're starting to succeed in new ways. The church world is watching and celebrating as this church that once had *it*, and started to lose *it*, got *it* back again.

WHAT CONTRIBUTES TO **it?**

Ready, Set, Fail

As you seek God and he rekindles *it* in your heart, I believe he is going to speak to you. Maybe he already has. He's directing you to step out of your comfort zone and do something in faith. Or if not now, he will soon. And when he does, mark my words, Satan will try to talk you out of *it*.

One of the enemy's greatest tools is fear. You might ask, "How do I overcome this fear of failure?" I like what my friend Mark Batterson says about fear: "The antidote for the fear of failure is not success but small doses of failure." Think about it. To keep you from getting the flu, what kind of shot does the doctor give you? He gives you a small dose of the flu. You get just enough to train your body to reject it. The same is true with failure. Once you fail and realize it's not the end of the world, you're not as afraid to fail again. Leo F. Buscaglia said it well: "We seem to gain wisdom more readily through our failures than through our successes. We always think of failure as the antithesis of success, but it isn't. Success often lies just the other side of failure."[30]

God gave me the great gift of failure early in the ministry. Much of what I tried failed. Our drama ministry fell apart. Our attempt at a choir didn't work. Our first mission trip didn't happen. Our Wednesday Bible study crashed before takeoff. Our monthly worship night happened only twice. Once, we tried a very simple sermon illustration during which Sam Roberts was supposed to toss me a football. We practiced dozens of times. On "game day" in front of the whole church, he threw a wild pass and I dove for it, missing the ball and crashing into the drum set. *Pass incomplete.* Much of what we tried failed.

Most people don't know how often we failed. One of the things our church is known for is meeting in multiple locations. But our first attempt at a video venue was a disaster. After struggling for four months, we pulled the plug. Three years ago we attempted two out-of-state campuses in the Phoenix area. It was a matter of months before we realized neither would survive. We were totally embarrassed. Not only did our whole church know about our failure, but so did many other church leaders who were watching. Even worse, we felt horrible about all the money we blew. This was God's money

and we flushed a lot of it down the drain. We tried, we failed, we learned, we adjusted, we combined the campuses, and we kept trying. It was an expensive and painful education. But it was a valuable one. What we learned from that failure would have been hard to learn any other way. We try to follow Irish writer Samuel Beckett's advice: "Go on failing. Go on. Only next time, try to fail better."[31] You could say we have failed our way to succeeding.

If you don't have *it*, maybe you need to try something new — and fail at it. I tell our staff often, "Fail! If you're not failing, you've stopped dreaming. You'll eventually stop learning. And you will stop growing."

Those who have *it*, fail often.

The Virtue of the Twice-Stung

The other day I was walking outside my house and got stung in the back of the head by a wasp. I cried like a four-year-old girl. Actually, most little girls would handle it better than I did. Now each time I walk by that same spot, I hesitate.

Too many ministry leaders are hesitant. And it's easy to understand why. They've tried something that didn't work as they expected it to. Then they faced ridicule, gossip, or maybe were even asked to leave their ministry roles. They've been stung once, and they go out of their way to avoid a repeat.

When you fail, you tend to second-guess yourself. *Maybe I didn't hear from God. Maybe I'm not gifted in ministry. Maybe I'll*

WHAT CONTRIBUTES TO it?

always fail. I don't think I have what it takes. Fight against that hesitant-leader syndrome. Sure, you'll want to be prayerful and wise as you move forward. Yes, you'll always want to consider the cost before launching a new ministry effort. But you must remember the words of the writer of Hebrews: "And without faith it is impossible to please God" (Heb. 11:6). God is calling you to risk being stung again. And again. And to recognize that this is the best way to live, the only way to please him.

If you're waiting for your venture to have guaranteed success, you'll probably be waiting for the rest of your life. Sometimes the fruit of your steps of faith is measured not so much by what God does *through* you as by what God does *in* you.

As I'm writing this chapter, I'm in the middle of a setback. Our church is experimenting with live video worship. And predictably, we're facing resistance. After all, it's new. Several years ago, we faced similar resistance to the idea of teaching on video. Very few people believed that mode of teaching would ever work. Years later, at our church most people prefer experiencing a video sermon over hearing the speaker in the flesh. But to get to this success, we had to work through the pain of resistance, technical growing pains, temporary failure, and our own self-doubts.

I have a similar theory about video worship. I believe it will work. And not just for our church but for churches around the world. Because there are more than three hundred thousand churches in our country, I know there is a big need for great worship leaders. Many churches simply don't have people with the gifts to lead worship. Because of this need, our church decided to offer free satellite worship to churches around the world. So last weekend we broadcast worship to four of our campuses. And according to most people, it didn't work well. In fact, many would say it failed. So we have a choice. We can surrender the idea and go off with our tails between our legs. Or we can thank God that he gave us the courage to try, learn from what happened, make some adjustments, and try again. Within a couple of years, I'm guessing we'll be providing very effective, anointed, and Spirit-filled worship to churches around the world.

Then again, maybe I'm wrong. But we'll never know until we try.

Dig Up Your Talent

Jesus told a story in Matthew 25 about three household managers whose master entrusted each of them with "talents" of money. (A talent was a unit of gold or silver, worth quite a bit in that day — not to be confused with our English word *talent*.) Two of the guys risked failure and invested their master's money. The third guy was afraid and refused to fail. He played it safe, avoided risk, and buried his talent — just like so many ministries do today.

Then the master came back and called his employees to report on their investments: "The man who had received the one talent [the guy who feared failure] came. 'Master,' he said, 'I knew that you are a hard man ... So I was *afraid* and went out and hid your talent in the ground. See, here is what belongs to you.'

"His master replied, 'You wicked, lazy servant! ... Take the talent from him and give it to the one who has the ten talents'" (Matt. 25:24 – 28, emphasis mine).

Luke 19 tells a similar story. *The Message* version offers this summary in verse 26: "Risk your life and get more than you ever dreamed of. Play it safe and end up holding the bag." Those who risked saw an increase. The one who played it safe lost it all.

What dream have you buried? What burden has God given you that you've put aside? Dig it up. Pull it out. Dust it off. It's time to start praying about your next risk. Is God calling you to start a new ministry? Maybe it's a Saturday evening worship experience? Maybe an outreach to inner-city kids? Maybe a new church? Or an internet ministry?

Is God calling you to take a chance on someone? To add to your ministry team someone who most think is unqualified? To reach out to someone who is far from God?

Or is God leading you to take a risk and shut down a dead ministry? Perhaps you know God wants you to have a tough conversation with someone. Or maybe he's leading you to find a new place to use your gifts.

Dig up your talent, the assets God has entrusted to you to use for his purposes. But remember, when you take a step of faith, the fear of failure might creep up on you, as it does with most people. *What if this doesn't work? What will people think? What if this bombs?* I can relate to all those fears. One of my mentors told me, "When you believe God is calling you to do something, you have to feel the fear and do it anyway" (my paraphrase).

Let God turn the fear into faith. Instead of becoming a hesitant leader, ask God to make you bold and aggressive.

Ministry without Regrets

When my son Sam was two years old, I stupidly put him on a scooter and let him ride down our steep driveway. He made several successful rides as I watched, beaming with pride, thinking, *Yep. A chip off the old block.*

On his final ride, Sam panicked and stepped off the scooter, snapping his femur clean in two. And it was my fault, a consequence of my poor judgment. He screamed and screamed in horror and pain. Little Sam spent the next six weeks in a full body cast. Once the cast was removed, it took him weeks to learn to walk again.

From that moment forward, Sam has been understandably terrified of the steep incline down the driveway. But a couple of years later, Sam bravely approached me and told me he *had* to ride the scooter down the driveway. I could tell he was paralyzed with fear but wanted to face and overcome it. I tried to talk him out if it, but he insisted. For quite some time he stood at the top of the driveway, crying quietly, breathing deeply, and preparing to face his greatest fear. Then he pushed off and soared down the driveway. He risked and won! I'd never

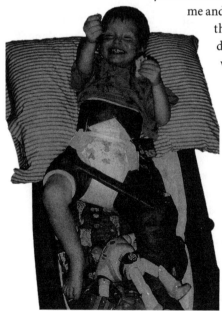

been more proud of him. That was a ride he had to take, a fear he had to conquer.

What ride do you need to take?

Learning to Fail Gracefully

Stuntmen and stuntwomen are paid to fall. They fall, get beat up, and get blown up ... gracefully. We need to learn to fail gracefully.

Because I've failed often, I've learned some principles about how to fail. Here are a few you might find helpful:

- *Call your new ideas "experiments."* Sometimes leaders make promises that they might not be able to deliver on. Instead of making absolute statements about what's coming, it helps to package new ventures as experiments. This gives the leaders some wiggle room to make minor tweaks or major adjustments. If the experiment doesn't work, we still come away with something valuable, something we've learned and can explain to those concerned.

- *Create a culture that allows failure.* Explain often that failure is a part of success. Talk openly about your failures and what you've learned. Explain that as a ministry, you're going to err on the side of being aggressive and failing occasionally, rather than being passive and succeeding at being average.

- *Don't internalize failures.* Remember that failure is an event, not a person. When you do fail, allow yourself to feel the disappointment. That's reality, and an important part of *it*. But don't internalize disapproval. Just because you failed at something doesn't mean you're a failure. Shake it off. And try something again.

- *Debrief after failures and successes.* After every new venture, take time to debrief. List the learning points. What worked? What didn't? What could you have done differently? What are the lessons you'll carry forward? Don't waste a setback by not learning from it.

- *Try again.* If you fall off your scooter, you have to get back on and ride again. Don't let yesterday's loss talk you out of tomorrow's win. Try again. God's not finished with you. Most big successes follow multiple failures. Failure is often the price you pay for success. Winston Churchill said, "Courage is going from failure to failure without losing enthusiasm."[32]

Get out of the Boat

Leaders with *it* know that their greatest fear is often the fear of failure. They also understand that their greatest pain one day will be regret for missed opportunities. So leaders are set up with a built-in avoidance of conflict reflex, and they must choose — consciously or unconsciously — which path they will avoid and, by default, which path they will choose. The *it*-rich are those who have chosen to face their fears rather than live with regrets.

When you lead on the edge, you'll learn to face your fears and conquer them, only to have new ones emerge. You'll learn that the illusion of security evaporates with your last accomplishment. But like Peter, you'll recognize that you're safer when you are out of the boat and *with Jesus* than if your fears kept you in the boat.

Get out of the boat. Face your fears. Fail. Learn. Adjust. Try again. And watch God do more than you can imagine.

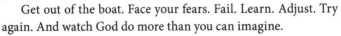

- Failure is not an option. It is a necessity.
- If you're not failing, you've stopped dreaming. You'll eventually stop learning. And you will stop growing. Those who have *it* fail often.
- Failure is often the tuition for success (adapted from Walter Brunell).
- Great leaders learn the art of failing forward.

it FACTORS

WHAT CONTRIBUTES TO it?

Questions for Discussion or Reflection

1 Describe the "failure culture" at your ministry. Is strategic failure strongly discouraged, quietly tolerated, or publicly embraced?

2 Is your ministry becoming more faith-filled or more risk-aversive? When is the last time you've taken a huge faith-risk? What happened? What did you learn?

3 *The Message* version of the Bible offers this summary in Luke 19:26: "Risk your life and get more than you ever dreamed of. Play it safe and end up holding the bag." In light of this verse, what is God saying to you about your ministry? How are you playing it safe? What risk is God calling you to take? What will you regret if you don't at least try?

4 Robert Schuller once asked, "What would you attempt if you knew it couldn't fail?" Talk with your team about this. If God would bless anything that you do, what would you attempt?

PROFILE

Mark Batterson
National Community Church
Washington, DC

> *The healthiest and holiest people are the people who laugh at themselves the most. Failure helps us take God more seriously and ourselves less seriously.*
>
> — **MARK BATTERSON**

On January 7, 1996, a blizzard left record amounts of snow on Washington, D.C. Only three people showed up for National Community Church's first worship experience: the pastor and church planter, Mark Batterson; his wife, Lora; and their son, Parker. Thankfully, the church grew more than 600 percent the next weekend when attendance skyrocketed to nineteen people.

After worshiping for a few months in a school, NCC moved to Union Station and started meeting in a movie theater. Tons of people started meeting Christ and the young church exploded with growth. Twelve years later, the church ministers to 1,500 each weekend in four locations and reaches an even larger audience through Mark's blog and podcasts. What is most amazing is that approximately 70 percent of NCCers come from an unchurched or "dechurched" background.

The casual observer might think that almost everything Mark has touched, God has blessed. Mark is the first to admit that most of the church's successes have followed a string of failures. In fact, Batterson humbly admits that before launching NCC, he tried to plant a church in Chicago that never materialized. His church had a name, a core group, and a bank account, but never made it to their first worship service. Batterson laughs when he reveals that he had a twenty-five-year plan, but no church.

This failure, although challenging at the time, was a gift in disguise. Mark realizes that failure isn't the end of the world. This early failure raised Mark's tolerance for pain and willingness to risk. Mark and his leaders swung for the fence in the spring of 2006, when NCC completed construction on Ebenezers, the largest coffeehouse on Capitol Hill. This unique coffeehouse is one block from Union Station; Batterson and his leaders created a place where the church and the community would intersect. Ebenezers is a fully operational coffeehouse open seven days a week and doubles as a place of worship on weekends.

Knowing full well the coffeehouse might not have made it through the first year, Mark credits his early failures with educating him to avoid the same mistakes and yet follow a spiritual entrepreneurial vision. Armed with humility from his previous failures, Mark's team devoted more time to prayer and depended on God. Mark says that his failures taught him that "'unless the Lord builds the house, the builders labor in vain' [Ps. 127:1]. Only God can build the church."

Batterson says, "Leaders need the courage to acknowledge when something isn't working. Over the years, we have killed services that weren't working. We've cut ministries that we felt were outside our calling. And we have discontinued lots of outreaches that weren't really making a difference."

The leaders of NCC fight against becoming what they call a closed system. They never want to limit their learning to what they know. The leaders of this innovative church refuse to do ministry from memory. Mark says, "Instead of repeating the past, these passionate people want to create the future, even if the creation is peppered with failures on the way to success."

When talking to pastors at leadership conferences, Mark encourages failure. He says, "The greatest thing that could happen to you is to fail at something, because you'll realize that God still loves you and he's there to pick you up and dust you off. Failure somehow relieves the pressure to succeed at everything."

Mark is quick to admit that failure is no fun when it is happening. But he says with a chuckle, "It is pretty funny after the fact!" And that includes the time NCC hosted their very first concert. The band had seven people playing to an audience of four. Mark laughed hard as he listed everything he learned from the bombed concert.

NINE

HEARTS FOCUSED OUTWARD:

YOU WANT OTHERS TO HAVE it

If your gospel isn't touching others, it hasn't
touched you.

—*Curry R. Blake*

What I saw years ago still breaks my heart. I was preaching for
a small church. The volunteer receptionist told me bluntly,
"Young man, you'd better do a good job preaching, because we
have a visitor coming to church." Evidently that was unusual. She
explained how a lady had just called and asked for directions to
the church. "Our church has been declining for several years,"
the receptionist said sadly, "and we need members to help pay
the bills."

Before the service started, I stood outside with a church elder
greeting people. That's when I saw *the visitor*. The reason I knew
this lady wasn't a member of the church was … well, because she
didn't look like anyone else there. All the members were dressed
in nice suits and pretty dresses. This young lady looked like she'd
slept in what she was wearing. It wasn't that she didn't care for herself; it was just obvious that she'd had a tough life. As she slowly

approached the church, her eyes and body language communicated she was nervous and intimidated. I admired her courage to visit a new church all by herself. What had triggered her to come? Had she been abused? Was she at the end of her rope and in desperate need of Christ and his people?

The elder stepped in front of the young lady and blocked her path into the sanctuary. "Miss," the man said in an intimidating tone, "at our church, we wear our best for God."

My jaw dropped in shock. *No! You didn't just say that to her.* Unfortunately, he had. This young woman's eyes filled with tears as she dashed to her car to make her getaway.

Heartbreaking.

I'd argue that people today aren't rejecting Christ so much as they're rejecting the church. Once, I asked a guy why he didn't go to church. He responded without hesitation, "Because I've already been."

He came. *It* didn't happen. So he never returned.

Have you ever visited a church and been overlooked? It makes you feel incredibly awkward, uncomfortable, and unwanted. What's odd is that churches that appear unfriendly to outsiders can be full of the friendliest people in the world. If you're an insider.

It-free churches are often very friendly. In fact, they can be so tight, so bonded, so close — to each other — that they unintentionally overlook those they don't know. On the other hand, ministries with *it* remember that Jesus came for outsiders. He came for those who were lost. Broken. Hurting. Disenfranchised. Alone. Overlooked. Poor. Jesus came for those whom religion rejected. Many churches unwittingly focus inward and forget those who are the very purpose for Jesus' coming, the very purpose for our being here on earth. These churches are like a hospital which no longer accepts patients. Or a soup kitchen which no longer feeds hungry people. Or like SpongeBob no longer wearing square pants. (I may have just given one metaphor too many there.)

Across the board, almost every with-*it* church I've observed is virtually obsessed with reaching those who don't know Christ. A passion to share Christ consumes them in a beautiful way. Without-*it* ministries can be filled with very sincere Bible-believing

Christians; unfortunately, they're simply more concerned about themselves than the lost.

Who Do You Love?

Once, a guy asked Jesus, "Of all the commands, what's the big one?"

Jesus replied, "'Love the Lord your God with all your heart and with all your soul and with all your mind and with all your strength.' The second is this: 'Love your neighbor as yourself'" (Mark 12:30 – 31, emphasis mine).

> 12 (Honour thy father and thy mother: that thy days may be long upon the land which the Lord thy God giveth thee.
> 13 Thou shalt not kill.
> 14 Thou shalt not commit adultery.
> 15 Thou shalt not steal.
> 16 Thou shalt not bear false witness against thy neighbour.
> 17 Thou shalt not covet thy neighbour's house, thou shalt not covet thy neighbour's wife,

Who do you love? If you love God, you should love people. If you don't love people, you don't love God. It's that simple. We're quite comfortable loving those who are like us, but we're also called to love those who *aren't* like us.

When we love deeply, love makes us do things we wouldn't otherwise do. For example, I'm a cheapo, but I'll spend big bucks on a date with my wife. What makes me do it? Love makes me do it.

Another example … I hate cats. My kids love cats. So we have two good-for-nothing, fur-ball-spitting, never-come-when-you-call-them cats. Why do I have two of something I hate? Because I love my kids. Love made me do it.

When one of my kids asked me yesterday for the cherry from my cherry limeade, I gave it to him. Again, love made me do it.

When my two-year-old pooped all over himself and my three-year-old saw it and then vomited her dinner of spaghetti with meatballs directly on the freshly squeezed poop, I cleaned it all up. What made me do it? Well, actually *Amy* made me do that, but you get the point.

Love makes you do crazy things. Who do you love? Do you love people who don't know Christ? The *it*-fueled do — and deeply. But honestly, many so-called Christians don't. You don't have to look far to find churches full of people who are insulating themselves from the world, hunkering down, avoiding PG-13 movies and secular music. These inward-looking religious types keep their distance from anyone who drinks beer, cusses after a bad golf swing, smokes anything, has a tattoo, or wears designer jeans with holes in them. They avoid homosexuals. They criticize rock stars. They stare disapprovingly at purple hair and mohawks. And they're afraid of MTV. Too many believers are avoiding "that kind" of person. And they've forgotten that Jesus came for that kind of person.

Do you love those who are without Christ? Be honest. Does your ministry have people whose hearts beat for those outside the family of God? Churches that have *it* care for each other *and* for people who are far from God. Churches and ministries without *it* care more about the sheep inside the fold than the goats outside of the church. And the lack of caring is communicated clearly. One church I visited has a beautiful stained-glassed window inscribed with the verse, "Jesus is the light of the world." The only problem is that the words are facing people inside the church instead of those who observe the message from the outside.

What caused the good shepherd to leave the ninety-nine to pursue the lost one? Love. What made the father stand on the edge of town praying that his lost son would return home? Love. What drove our heavenly Father from heaven to earth? Love again. John 3:16 records his motivation: "For God so *loved* the world that he gave his one and only Son, that whoever believes in him shall not perish but have eternal life" (emphasis mine).

Do you love the lost?

An Open-Roof Policy

Life in Palestine in Jesus' day was very public. People generally left their doors open during the day. An open door meant anyone could enter.

One day in Capernaum, Jesus started teaching inside an open-doored house, and his followers barged right on in. Soon the tiny house was packed like sardines and people overflowed into the streets. (Jesus could have gone to two services or started a second campus. Too bad we weren't there to advise him.)

We know that out of the entire crowd, at least four guys got *it*. These fanatical four had a crippled friend who desperately needed Jesus. They weren't on a mission to get Jesus to autograph their "Jesus is my homeboy" T-shirts. They were on a mission to get their friend to Christ.

What about the rest of the crowd? Some were probably very sincere in their desire to hear Jesus. Others might have been skeptical, hoping to prove Jesus was a fake. But four guys were thinking about someone else. Even though the others might have hung on Jesus' words, many missed the heart of his message. Jesus came not for the healthy but for the sick.

For the crowd, the meeting was about them. What could they get? What could they learn? What could Jesus offer them? Churches without *it* are filled with well-meaning Christians with similar attitudes. You can hear it in their self-centered words:

- We love this church because it is convenient for us.
- We go to this church because our kids love the day care.
- This church makes me feel better about myself.

You can hear it in their language when they are searching for a church home. "We're church shopping," they might say. We know what they mean, but their words imply that they're consumers looking for some church to meet their needs. When they find a church they like, they join it. If one day this church no longer meets their needs, they leave, singing the national anthem of consumeristic church hoppers: "We're just not getting fed. We're not getting fed. We're going to leave every church in town and we won't stop until we're dead." Erwin McManus asked, "When have we forgotten that the church doesn't exist for us? We are the church and we exist for the world."

Turning Outward

If your ministry has become focused on the already-convinced, I'll bet that your ministry doesn't have *it*. You're not likely seeing many, if any, conversions. Baptisms are few and far between. Membership classes are tiny. You're not experiencing great works of the Spirit of God. New people aren't coming and staying. Longtime members aren't growing. Things may be stable, but they're stagnant; you're not seeing forward movement.

We can learn a few things from these four men. For starters, to have *it*, we have to care about those who are far from God. Many people don't.

Tony Campolo tells a story about a preacher correcting his inward-looking church. "The problem," the preacher's voice boomed, "is that people are dying all over the world and you don't even give a damn!" When he punched the final word, the crowd gasped. Women looked at each other, stunned. Kids sat at attention, afraid to budge. The elders eyed one another, sending silent but understood messages: *We have to meet. Soon.*

The minister continued, much more slowly and with obvious pain, "The saddest part is ..." He paused and started again. "The saddest part is that most of you are more upset that I used the word *damn* in church than you are that people are dying and going to hell."

Ouch.

Do you care about those who are without Christ? Before you give me the programmed Sunday-school answer most ministers give, let me help you answer this question honestly.

- When is the last time you've had a lost person in your home? (The plumber who repaired your sink doesn't count.)
- How many meaningful conversations did you have with non-Christians this week?
- Who are the nonbelievers you prayed for today?

WHAT CONTRIBUTES TO it?

If you can't answer those questions with several names, chances are you're on the road to not caring. Or perhaps you've already arrived and have settled in at that dangerous destination. To be fair, most Christians don't wake up one morning and declare, "I've decided not to care about the lost anymore." The attitude creeps in over time. After being a Christian for a few years, we don't have a ton in common with non-Christians, so we don't typically develop quality relationships. Over time, many Christ-followers realize they have almost no relationships with unbelievers.

If that's you, ask God to increase your heart for those without Christ. He will. Before long, God will send you someone — maybe a bunch of someones — whom you'll care about. Your love for them will increase. When that happens, you get *it*, and *it*'s almost impossible to turn off. Your prayer life increases. You're looking for opportunities to shift conversations toward spiritual things. You're ever aware that you're representing Christ. When you have *it*, people tend to want it. Your passion for Christ is contagious.

I bumped into two wonderfully obnoxious guys last week. Unquestionably, they have *it*. Both guys talked simultaneously, describing the Bible study they were having in a restaurant. After too many refills of Diet Coke, these two went to the men's room and were talking about Jesus while "taking care of business." Two other guys overheard their conversation. Before long, these bathroom evangelists led the other two guys in a prayer to know Christ — right in the men's bathroom. (It is amazing where God will work and what he'll do when we follow his lead.) Their new friends followed them and enjoyed the remainder of the Bible study. Now the new believers are regulars at the study gatherings.

For too many years I was not focused on sharing Christ. Like many, I was consumed with my own problems. Life became about me. When I reconnected with Christ, he reignited my evangelistic flame. Now that I have *it* again, God almost seems to be bringing people to me to share with. Just yesterday I was at the gym talking to a trainer. This guy knows I'm a pastor but doesn't know he probably shouldn't use the f-bomb around me. He drops cuss words like Eminem drops rhymes. Even though I was ready to work out, I could tell he needed to talk. In the past, I might've been selfish and politely brushed him off so I could commence sweating. But somehow I knew God wanted me to continue the conversation with this guy.

Moments later, the trainer, whom I barely knew, shared how his girlfriend had cheated on him. Before I could bring up anything spiritual, he asked if I'd pray for him. After our prayer, I talked to him about Christ. He was curious but had some reservations about Christianity because of a bad experience with some Christians. I invited him to church this weekend. He said, "That's what I need to do."

If you're a leader of your ministry, you need to recognize that, for better or for worse, your ministry reflects you. If you don't care about Christless lives, the people you lead aren't likely to care. Well-known preaching professor Howard Hendricks said, "In the midst of a generation screaming for answers, Christians are stuttering."[33]

Lessons from Four Home-Wreckers

Many of our churches unintentionally turn their backs on those who need Jesus most. We focus inward. We do our Bible studies. We listen to our favorite Christian music. We watch our Christian shows. We speak our Christianese. *(Praise the Lord, brother. Thank God I'm blood-bought, sanctified, Spirit-filled, and glory bound!)* And we're basically saying to those who need him most, "You can just go to hell." Okay, so I know that's not what we're actually saying, but if we're not careful, that's what our uncaring attitudes will communicate.

Here are a few things that the fervent, fixated, friend-toting four of Capernaum teach us. First, they recognized their friend needed Jesus. Too many believers forget that the lost *really* need

WHAT CONTRIBUTES TO **it**?

Jesus. You can see it in what I call "good-old-boy theology." I can't tell you how many times I've visited a family in which someone just passed away and I ask about their deceased loved one. The family shuffles back and forth awkwardly before saying, "Well, Grandpa wasn't much of churchgoer and he definitely wasn't religious, but he was a hard worker, and besides his gambling problem and the fact that he ordered himself a strip-o-gram for his eightieth birthday, he was a pretty moral person. We know he's in a better place."

We want to believe that people we love never go to hell. We can always talk ourselves into believing people are better off now that they're dead, and it lessens our urgency to reach those without Christ.

We also see that it took four different people to get this one to Jesus. A church that has *it* recognizes that reaching people is not just the pastor's job. It's *everyone's* job. I can't do it alone. You can't do it alone. It takes all of us.

If you're anything like me, you might feel nervous in spiritual conversations. In seminary I took a class on personal evangelism. We had to go door-to-door and knock and try to lead the unsuspecting person — who was probably traumatized by being faced with some young seminarian ready to talk about hell while a teacher looked over his shoulder to grade him — to Christ. My professor always reminded us to pray before we knocked. I always pleaded, "God, I pray no one is home!" Why? Because I was nervous. I never felt like I'd do it right.

We have to remember, we do our part, others do their part, and God does his. We're never the answer; Jesus always is. I know many churches that are afraid to ask people to follow Christ. The leaders are afraid no one will respond. I always tell young ministers, "You don't fail if the Spirit prompts you to ask someone to follow Christ and the person doesn't. You fail when the Spirit prompts you but you're afraid to ask." Don't blame yourself if someone rejects Jesus. That's putting yourself in God's place. And the flip side of that attitude is the temptation to take credit when someone accepts Jesus.

Outreach is a team event. You might be just one of the four. Your position might be pray-er. Or conversationalist. Or simply love-of-Jesus-style good-doer. God might put you in for the first quarter, then bench you while others perform their specialties. You do your part. Let others do theirs. And watch God do his.

Cutting through the Crap

The four guys with *it* were determined to do everything necessary to get their crippled friend to Jesus. As they approached the home, they couldn't get in because the crowd was way too big. Undeterred by that little problem, the four amigos decided to bust him in, so they climbed up on the roof of the house. The roofs on these homes typically were flat with beams about three feet apart. The gaps between the beams were covered with brush and clay and packed with manure. You read that right ... manure.

Imagine the scene: Jesus is teaching. I mean, he's in the flow, on a roll, movin' with the Spirit. A flake of dried poop lands on his nose. He looks up and the ceiling starts caving in. The home owner is not exactly pleased. Suddenly the light of the sun explodes through a big hole, shining around the silhouettes of four guys leaning over and staring down at everyone. Jesus starts laughing with delight.

These guys were willing to bust through any barriers. They even cut through the manure.

Churches that have *it* are filled with people who sincerely desire to reach the lost. And they won't let any excuses stop them. Crowd blocking the path? No problem. They'll go over, under, around, or through it. Roof in the way? Nothing stands in the way of *it*. They'll cut through the roof.

Love overcomes the obstacles.

The very first thing Jesus did was to heal the crippled man's greatest injury. Jesus forgave his sins. Then Jesus said to the paralytic, "'I tell you, get up, take your mat and go home.' He got up, took his mat and walked out in

WHAT CONTRIBUTES TO it?

full view of them all. This amazed everyone and they praised God, saying, 'We have never seen anything like this!' " (Mark 2:11 – 12).

You know your ministry has *it* when people start talking like the people in this story. They tell everyone, "We've never seen anything like this!"

Shifting the Focus Outward

If your ministry doesn't have *it* and you want it, shifting to an outward, evangelistic focus is essential. Let's keep things simple. What does it take for you to see people come to Christ? I'd say three things:

1. People who don't know Christ
2. A clear explanation of the gospel story
3. Genuine faith

Let's break these down to see the importance of each. First, to see people come to Christ in your ministry, you'll need to have those who don't know him present. If people far from God aren't coming to your church, you'll want to identify why. Some reasons could include:

- Your people don't have relationships with the lost.
- Your people are too embarrassed to bring their friends to church.
- Your building and/or people are subtly communicating "stay away."

Do whatever it takes to make your ministry a place that welcomes those who don't know Christ.

Second, you must have a clear presentation of Jesus' story. If all your messages are simply "how to have a better life" type of messages, don't expect people to be saved. Too many messages contain more self-help than gospel. I like the idea of offering simultaneous comfort and confrontation. John 1:14 says that Jesus was full of grace and truth. Our ministries should reflect these qualities. At the same moment we're welcoming someone with a comfortable environment and friendly people, we want to confront them lovingly with truth. If someone doesn't recognize her sin, she'll never crave a savior. I suggest inviting people to follow Christ every time you meet.

Finally, you need real faith. If you don't *really* believe in the power of Christ to change a life, people will know. The opposite is true as well. If you believe with every fiber in your body that Christ can and will instantly transform a life, people will sense it, feel it, and may believe it as well.

So You Think You Have *It*

You may have read this chapter and thought, *I'm a part of a very evangelistic ministry.* Thankfully today we're witnessing many churches seeing dozens, hundreds, even thousands finding Christ. If that's you, I praise God with you. But here is a quick caution. Let's not boast in something that isn't ours to boast in. Ultimately, we preach, we pray, we invite, we believe, and Christ changes lives.

When we start to measure *our* success by *God's* performance, we're treading on dangerous ground. I try to take the viewpoint of the veteran rescue diver, played by Kevin Costner, in the movie *The Guardian.* At the end of the movie, the up-and-coming hot-shot diver asks the retiring legendary diver, "What's your number?" He wants to know how many rescues the record holder carries. The young and competitive diver is assuming he'll hear two or three hundred rescues.

Instead, Costner's character replies, "What's my number? My number is twenty-two."

The young guy is shocked. "Twenty-two," he says with great disappointment. "I thought you'd saved many more than that."

The veteran looks back over his shoulder and says, "Twenty-two is the number of people that I lost. That's the only number I ever counted."

Instead of boasting in how many people we've seen saved, those who have *it* realize how many more God wants to reach.

WHAT CONTRIBUTES TO *it*?

- When we love deeply, love makes us do things we wouldn't otherwise do.
- To have *it*, we have to care about those who are far from God. Many people don't.
- When our churches look inward instead of outward, we're basically saying to nonbelievers, "You can just go to hell."
- Be careful not to blame yourself if someone rejects Christ. If you do, you might be tempted to take credit when someone accepts him.
- Love overcomes obstacles.

it FACTORS

Questions for Discussion or Reflection

1 Do you love those who don't know Christ? What about the leaders of your church? On a scale of one to ten (ten being the highest), what is the evangelistic temperature of your church? Are you willing to lose some people from your church to reach those without Christ?

2 What are you doing to reach the lost? When is the last time you had a lost person in your home? Talk about the most recent spiritual conversation you had with a nonbeliever. Who are you praying for to receive Christ?

3 Is your church focused more outward or inward? Would a guest clearly understand the gospel after attending your church for one month? Would you bring a nonbeliever to your church every week? Why or why not? If you said no, discuss what needs to change.

4 A great evangelistic ministry should offer both comfort and confrontation. Is your ministry more comforting or confronting? What do you need to do better to offer a balance of grace and truth?

WHAT CONTRIBUTES TO **it**?

> *Central is also a place where it's okay not to be okay. You don't have to fake perfection. Just come as you are with your past, pain, challenges, and junk. God promises to meet you where you are, but he won't leave you there.*
>
> — **JUD WILHITE**

In 2003 at the age of thirty-two, Jud Wilhite followed Gene Apple as the pastor of Central Christian Church in Las Vegas, Nevada. Under his leadership, the church has grown from 7,000 people to more than 13,000 people in three short years and was named by *Outreach* magazine as the twentieth fastest-growing church in America in 2007.

Jud explains the heart behind his leadership, which has helped create a church that is focused outward. "First, there is the biblical text, particularly the book of Acts, which paints a picture of the faith community with a passionate concern to spread God's fame to the world. The more we deal with the text as a community, the more it drives us to be focused outward. We ask, 'How can we serve our community?' In serving them with openness and honesty, we'll have opportunities to share our faith."

Jud often reminds his church family to remember where they've come from and how God's grace has changed their lives. Remembering how God has transformed them encourages the members to share that same grace with others, especially in the broken city of Las Vegas.

Jud lights up with enthusiasm when he inspires others to "put skin on" their outward-focused hearts. He explains, "We motivate our people to be praying for one friend or family member every day who is far from God. We write their names down. We talk about them often. We say every one of us has one life and everyone can influence at least one life. From service planning to creative meetings, we are always wiring things up for specific people and asking, 'How would my friend Tom, who is not a Christian, respond to this?'"

Jud is quick to remind other leaders that changing a church culture can take years and a lot of hard work, and yet with deep passion, he reminds them that it is always worth it. He suggests:

- Start creating a culture of storytelling, in which people are inspired by the difference Jesus makes.
- Get discussions going with volunteers about their friends and family members and brainstorm ways to help people take steps closer to God.
- Remind your church that it is one of the only institutions that exists for those who are not already a part of it.
- Ask yourself and your leaders, "If our church packed up and moved out of our city, what difference would it make?" Then let that motivate you to make a difference.

When I asked Jud to tell me about someone whose life was changed, the stories flowed with passion. There is an ultimate fighter named Jake. He became a follower of Christ at Central, and now he prays with all the fighters before going into the cage. There's Gabriella, the woman who bottomed out after a tough divorce and numerous medical expenses. When she couldn't pay the bills, she decided to work the streets as a prostitute to support her kids. When the church reached out to her family and gave her child school supplies, she felt God had not abandoned her. She went on to become a follower of Jesus, and the church helped her find work and get back on her feet. And then there is BeBe, a delightful eighty-year-old woman filled with spunk. When she found Christ, she gave her pastor a big hug and said, "Jud, I have been lost for eighty years of my life, and I have just now found my way!"

TEN

KINGDOM-MINDEDNESS:

YOU SHARE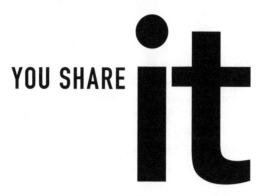

What we do for ourselves dies with us. What we do for others and the world remains and is immortal.

—Albert Pine

recently I bumped into an older lady who recognized me as the pastor of LifeChurch.tv. She explained that she was a member of another church in town. Although I didn't know her pastor well, I expressed that I'd heard a lot of great things about him. She responded soberly, "Wow! I can't believe you're speaking well of the competition." Shocked, I explained that in no way did I view her church as a competitor. She shot back, "Your church is unquestionably the competition. We're fighting to make sure we get as many members as we can before you and other churches get them all." I had no idea how to respond, so I punched her in the face, breaking her nose.

Okay, I didn't punch her, but God's heart must break over that kind of attitude. Jesus said in Luke 11:17, "Any kingdom divided against itself will be ruined, and a house divided against itself will fall." Seventeenth-century Puritan minister Richard Baxter echoed Jesus' sentiment when he lamented, "Is it not enough that all the world is against us, but we must also be against one another? O happy days of persecution, which drove us together in love, whom the sunshine of liberty and prosperity crumbles into dust by our contentions!"[34]

The more possessive and competitive we are, the more divided we become. Virtually every ministry I've ever known that had *it* was not divisive. The leaders were kingdom-minded.

What do I mean by kingdom-minded?

A kingdom-minded ministry is one whose leaders care more about what God is doing everywhere than what God is doing in their own ministry. A kingdom-minded ministry is generous and eager to partner with others to get more done for the glory of God.

It's hard to have *it* without desiring that other ministries succeed. When you have *it*, you know that it doesn't belong to you. *It* belongs to God. He gives *it*. And since *it* is his and not yours, you're willing to share *it*.

Those who have *it* know *it* is not about them. *It* is not about their personal names. *It* is not about Willow Creek Community Church. *It* is not about North Point, Elevation Church, NewSpring Church, Mars Hill, Vintage Faith, First Baptist, Wesley United Methodist, Lord of Life Lutheran, Holy Ghost Temple of Righteous Praise, or whatever your church is called. *It* is not about *your* student ministry, *your* children's ministry, *your* new logo or website. And *it* is certainly not about your name. *It* is about Jesus. There's no other name under heaven that's anywhere close to his name. *It's* all about him.

I learned this the hard way. There was one particular year in our church when we definitely didn't have *it*. This happened to be the year our church didn't grow. I think we didn't grow because we had lost focus — *I* had lost focus — and *it* blurred, faded, and disappeared.

One weekend that year, I was driving between our two campuses to speak. Each time I'd take the trip, I'd pass several churches on the journey. By the looks of one church's empty parking lot, I assumed that church had very few people attending. With a com-

bination of pride and pity, I prayed, *God, help this little church. I pray you would bless them and they'd reach a ton of new people.*

As I was praying, I felt like God asked me a question. *Craig, would you be excited if their growth exceeded yours?*

And my honest answer was ... no.

That's hard for me to admit. No, I wouldn't have been happy if this church outgrew ours. It wasn't that I didn't want them reaching people; I just wanted to reach more. No matter how you slice that apple, I was territorial, insecure, and self-centered. Instead of having a heart for God's kingdom, I had a desire to build my kingdom — and God simply won't bless that. He shouldn't. And I think that's why we weren't growing. If I were God, I wouldn't have grown our church either.

Napoleon Bonaparte once said, "I am surrounded by priests who repeat incessantly that their kingdom is not of this world and yet they lay their hands on everything they can get." Do you know any pastors like that? We say our church or ministry is not about us. But for many of us, that's all we can talk about or think about. Not only is our kingdom not of this world, but to build our own is surely one of the grossest sins. After I recognized my sinful attitudes, my prayers started to change. *God, make me more generous. Expand my heart for others. Make me truly a kingdom-minded leader.*

As pastors and Christian leaders, we should be thrilled when other ministries succeed. It's odd to me how much easier it is to be pumped for those who are growing in another town. *Yeah God! I'm thrilled their ministry in that other state is growing!* If they're in my town, it's easy to feel threatened or competitive. *What? The church down the street is doing well? They must be preaching a feel-good message.* That attitude is wrong. It's dangerous.

I'd go so far as to say that God won't let a ministry keep *it* for long if they won't give *it* away. Keeping *it* to yourself is a sure way to kill *it*. And those ministries that don't have much of *it* often work hard to guard what little of *it* they have. What's funny about *it* is the more you try to hoard *it*, the less of *it* you tend to have. The more you are willing to give *it* away, the more of *it* God seems to give.

I Was Willing to Take from Others, But ...

Have you ever had one of those times when you were preparing a message, but God seemed to be playing the "silent game"? It was a Saturday night sometime in the first year of our church, hours before I was supposed to preach, and I had nothing. I prayed, read my Bible, and prayed some more. Sometimes when I'm preparing, God empowers the process, almost like he's inspiring every word. Other times, it's like he doesn't even exist.

Panic. Desperation. *God, where* are *you?* Please *give me something worthwhile to share. I promise I'll study better, be nicer to my wife, give more money, and take that trip to Africa I've been avoiding.*

Then I did it. (For years I had heard of those who did it, but I'd never done it.) Rather, I let someone else do it ... share *it*. I listened to a Rick Warren message, reworked it some, added my own illustrations, and preached it the next day. *Gasp.* To my surprise, God blessed it and used it. I suddenly learned to lean on those who had gone before me.

Rick Warren and Bill Hybels helped teach me to preach. With little experience teaching God's Word, I was doomed to lay some eggs. (If you're not a preacher, that means to preach some sucky sermons.) Both of these humble giants spoke into my life and into the lives of everyone who was attending LifeChurch.tv in its

WHAT CONTRIBUTES TO it?

infancy. Most amazing, these guys didn't even know. Certainly their messages ministered to me, but that's not what I mean. I listened to these men, borrowed from them, made their messages my own, and after giving them credit, I preached "our" messages.

When I inevitably discovered Fellowship Church and North Point Church, Ed Young and Andy Stanley each opened my eyes to different ways to do ministry. Their insight taught me how to harness my renewed mind and how to be creative spiritually. I occasionally borrowed their titles, phrases, and points, and then used them at my church to reach more people than I could have on my own. (The only problem is I don't look as cool as Andy looks sitting at a table, and I can't pull off wearing the shirts Ed wears.)

Many of the great communicators invite other ministers to use their messages. During my early years of ministry, I benefited countless times from others' hard work. Standing on the shoulders of great communicators and leaders, while submitting to God's fresh direction, I was empowered by God to reach more people than I ever dreamed possible.

Then one day I heard about a guy who preached one of *my* series. *The low-down, no-good, sermon-stealing, pathetic jerk of a preacher! How could he do that? That's my sermon!*

When I mouthed off to a friend about this, he gently reminded me that I did the same thing.

He was right. I was willing to take from others but unwilling to be generous with what I wrongly called mine. Then he told me that I should be honored and thrilled that someone would compliment my work in such a way.

My wise friend was dead on the money. God quickly changed my heart from being defensive and territorial to being more kingdom-minded. I was so pumped. What a gracious honor! Did I *really* produce something someone else could use? Was it possible for other preachers to benefit from *my* studying, as I had benefited from theirs? I prayed, *God, please use me to help other pastors the way you've used other pastors to help me.*

If you're looking to find more of *it* in your ministry, maybe you should look for more ways to give whatever part of *it* you have to others. That's what I've been learning and becoming increasingly passionate about with each passing day.

Sharing *It*

Have you ever asked yourself, What would happen if churches *really* worked together? Vesta Kelly said, "Snowflakes are one of nature's most fragile things, but just look at what they can do when they stick together."[35] Think of what believers could do if we partnered together. Instead of being jealous, territorial, or easily threatened, what if we became dangerously generous with our resources, ideas, and ministries? Do you think God would up your *it*?

Like some, I grumbled and griped because few practice kingdom generosity, but I never did anything about it. I was selfish. I wanted others to be generous and helpful, yet I wasn't. Then God's Spirit changed my heart.

Having learned from others, I wanted to pass along the wealth. As our church grew, more people asked for our ideas and support. One of the most common things churches asked was to use our videos, artwork, and creative elements and messages. As demand increased, we were tempted to sell our resources to increase revenue. More money means more ministry — certainly nothing's wrong with that. Every church I know that sells their messages and creative content uses the profits to reach more people. They have massive organizations, with overhead and employees, providing valuable, affordable resources. More power to them.

Like other churches, we wanted to help other ministries around the world, but launching a division to do that didn't fit our vision. We prayed, *Lord, how can we partner with other ministries, without wasting your time and money, to advance your kingdom?*

Eventually God gave us a crazy idea — one that just might work. What if, we asked idealistically, we just gave away our creative content? We had some hard discussions. Clearly, God was calling us to take this leap of faith. Although building the systems, supporting the bandwidth, and managing the site would cost something, the investment was minuscule compared with the potential spiritual dividends. LifeChurch.tv Open was born.

Some of our team members worried that if we gave away our stuff, we might lose *it*. If someone else had some of what we consider special, wouldn't that diminish our impact? We quickly discovered that the opposite is true. The more we gave away, the more God used the same resources in other places, and instead of depleting our creative ideas, we discovered more. The more of *it* we gave away, the more of *it* God gave back.

The self-centered ministry generally loses *it*. And the kingdom-minded ministry seems to attract *it*. As you become more generous, God likely will increase your impact and reach. As your influence expands, you likely will attract better leaders, pastors, and creative ministers.

As your library of ministry material grows, you might consider doing the same thing. Or not. You could sell what you have with integrity. And that might be the right way for you to go. With the proceeds, you could dig water wells for the thirsty, build homes for orphans, pay for your television outreach, or plant churches. Or you might consider something completely different, maybe only recently possible because of technology. Maybe you could take what you've already created, spend just a little more, and make it available. Then give as much of it away as possible.

If you choose to share *it*, here's what I believe will happen:

- *You'll help pastors do better ministry.* It's thrilling. Pastors from around the world, in churches of every size, have contacted us to say they're benefiting from what we've already created. In the first month after launching LifeChurch.tv Open with no advertising whatsoever, more than one thousand churches in eleven countries downloaded more than ten thousand pieces from the site.
- *You'll develop kingdom partnerships.* We're making friends with leaders we wouldn't have met otherwise. Our friendships are growing and we're working together to find staff, share ideas, and even partner to plant new campuses and churches.

- *You'll model effective stewardship.* You'll extend the life of your creative material. If you preach a sermon once, it's used once. If you give it away, it might be used fifty times. If five hundred people attend your church, and you spend five hundred dollars on staff and the use of equipment to make a video, then that video's cost is one dollar per person. But if just ten other churches use that same video, and each has 150 members, then you've dramatically reduced the cost to just twenty-five cents per person. Any pastor will tell you that God honors that kind of sensible faithfulness.

- *You'll encourage others to radical generosity.* Almost immediately after our launching LifeChurch.tv Open, several other churches followed suit.

- *God will bless you with more of* it. It might be more creative, biblical content and ideas. It could be generous givers or evangelistic leaders. God might send you more people who don't know Christ. The bottom line is that when you give *it*, God gives *it* back to you. As we've shared the ideas God has shared with us, he's sparked even more. Who's more creative than the Creator?

- *When you share* it, *kingdom unity emerges.* The things that divide us become less important. We all share our humanity, our fallenness. When we see others being real about who they are, we are drawn together, and we are more likely to help each other, more likely to share our other resources.

- *Really, you can't imagine what will happen.* Only God can see the whole picture. Just as a certain message, a certain song, a certain turn of phrase can surprise you by sparking life-changing power in people, we often don't know what God's trying to do until we take a risk. If we truly believe that we are his people, that this is his world, and if we trust in his concept of eternity, not ours, then what do we really have to lose?

John Wesley said it well: "Do all the good you can. By all the means you can, in all the ways you can, in all the places you can,

WHAT CONTRIBUTES TO **it?**

OPEN.LifeChurch.tv
free resources for churches

Message Series, Artwork Files,
Small Groups Content, Youth &
Kids Content, and Ministry
Tools...all of it is FREE!

Come and discover what you
can do through OPEN.

open.lifechurch.tv

at all the times you can, to all the people you can, as long as you ever can." Churches with *it* model his vision. They know we can do far more together than we can apart.

Other Ways to Share *It*

Whenever God blesses your ministry, I pray you'll be hungry to partner with others. Whatever he gives you, share *it*. Here are some other ideas of how you might be able to become more kingdom-minded.

Ask yourself what you can give away. I know several churches who provide a free CD and DVD ministry. These generous churches offer their weekend messages free to anyone who will give them as gifts to individuals. This is relatively inexpensive and can spread the Word to people and other ministries.

I also deeply admire some ministries that are sharing buildings. Ask yourself if you have a nice building or even a room that goes unused on Saturday nights or some other time. Maybe you could offer the use of your facility free to a church plant or an international church that meets sometime in the week when you're not using it. Or the new church plant might buy you a new sound system or video projector in exchange for using your building. With careful planning and good communication, everyone wins.

How about taking up an offering for another ministry? Suppose another church in your town undertakes a building project. Receive an offering and send it to them. Your church can model kingdom generosity and help the family of Christ.

You can also commit to speak well of other ministries. To embrace others, you have to acknowledge that your way of doing ministry is not the only way, or even the best way. If everyone did ministry the way you do, we'd never reach the world. You can decide never to talk badly about another Christian leader or church. Work to brag on other ministries, especially in your own community.

Think about ways to partner with other churches and ministries. Well over three hundred thousand American churches are trying to do separate mission work. What if you partnered with another church (or two or twenty) to make a difference in one significant place? It just might end the days when you find yourself canceling mission trips because of a lack of interest. Instead, your trips will overflow with participants and you'll have to book more.

Maybe your church can't afford a full-time singles pastor. Consider bringing four or five churches together for monthly singles events. All the churches can still minister to their adult singles and maybe reach some new people. Some of the singles might even thank you when they find godly wives or husbands.

As God gives *it* to you, give *it* away. (If it helps to motivate you, just sing the lyrics of the Red Hot Chili Peppers' song "Give It Away," which says, "Give it away, give it away, give it away now" over and over again, followed by "ooh … ooh yeah.") Remember where you find *it*? You find *it* in people! One of the most generous gifts you can give is the gift of people. You might prayerfully send individuals or families with spiritual gifts, or just wonderful hearts, to other churches. One weekend, I promoted ten other churches. I gathered their brochures and told our church, "If you aren't making a difference or growing spiritually at LifeChurch.tv, try one of these." Then I described some of the strengths of each one. Many people took me up on that challenge and later wrote me thank-you notes. We cleared some needed seats to reach more people, and the other churches in town were grateful.

WHAT CONTRIBUTES TO **it?**

We have even been honored by several churches who've called and said in effect, "We don't have *it*, but we want *it*. Can we merge ministries?" We've partnered with four churches that decided to become a part of LifeChurch.tv. Across the country, many ministries are realizing they can do more united than they can divided.

Be generous with *it*! Find a church that could benefit from what you're doing and adopt them. What does that mean? I'm not sure. You prayerfully decide. How can you help? Maybe your leaders can mentor theirs. Maybe you can give them your old choir robes or your church van. You might help them find the worship leader they're looking for. Whatever it means to you, do it.

As church leaders, we should continually ask, "What do we have that could benefit the kingdom?" I promise you that God has given you something valuable.

It could be your:

Time

Ideas

People

Talent

Buildings

Reputation

Finances

Blog

Remember the lady I told you about at the beginning of the chapter? The one who said our church was her church's competition? I bumped into her again several months later. She approached me humbly and said, "I think I owe you an apology." She explained how her pastor was using some of our resources and how excited he was to partner with us to reach people. She smiled from ear to ear and hugged me, fighting back the tears as she said, "Thank God we're on the same team."

Whatever you have, remember *it* is not yours. *It* belongs to God. And he wants you to give *it* away. Then watch as God stretches *it*, multiplies *it*, and spreads *it* around!

What can you do? More than you think.

- The more possessive and competitive we are, the more divided we become.
- A kingdom-minded ministry is more about what God is doing everywhere than what God is doing in your own ministry.
- A kingdom-minded ministry is generous and hungry to partner with others to get more done for the glory of God.
- When you have *it*, you know that *it* doesn't belong to you. *It* belongs to God. He gives *it*. Since *it* is his and not yours, you're willing to share *it*.
- The more you try to keep *it*, the less of *it* you tend to have. The more you are willing to give *it* away, the more of *it* God seems to give.

it FACTORS

Questions for Discussion or Reflection

1 Do you see other ministries as teammates or as competitors? When a new church or a similar ministry starts close to you, do you feel excited, or threatened? Why? What can you do to train your mind to be focused on the kingdom rather than focused inward?

2 Would you be thrilled if God blessed a smaller ministry down the road more than he is blessing yours? Why or why not?

3 Is your leadership focused more on building your ministry or on building God's kingdom? What can you do as leaders to become more kingdom-minded? What can you do to help other local churches? What do you have that you could give to another ministry? How can you promote kingdom unity with your words?

4 Alan Redpath said: "Before we can pray, 'Lord, Thy Kingdom come,' we must be willing to pray, 'My Kingdom go.' "[36] How do you think God wants to expand his kingdom through you? Is there any part of your ministry that is more your kingdom than God's kingdom? What in your heart or actions needs to change?

Dino Rizzo

Healing Place Church

Baton Rouge, Louisiana

> We are here not only to help people in our community but also to help other pastors and churches as they get started. It seems like that's really the way it should be. We are blessed to be a blessing however we can. If there's something we have that they need, we want to do all we can to give it to them.
>
> — DINO RIZZO

Of all the Christian leaders I've met, I don't know one who is more kingdom-minded than Dino Rizzo, pastor of Healing Place Church in Baton Rouge, Louisiana. Healing Place was founded in 1993 and ministers to 6,100 people weekly at their church. But their impact is felt way beyond just their church. Because of Dino's generous spirit, the people in his church are making a difference around the world.

When I asked Dino to share some of what they do to help others, he rattled off more examples than I could list. I'll give you a few. Healing Place Church habitually shares relief or outreach supplies to places around the world. They send anything from truckloads of bananas to boxes of diapers and crates of Snapple. When tragedy strikes a community, Healing Place people are often close by.

WHAT CONTRIBUTES TO IT?

The church sent cooking teams to New York and the Pentagon after September 11th and medical mobiles to help those impacted by Hurricane Ivan, and the church served as a hub connecting churches from around the world after Hurricane Katrina.

Dino expresses a sincere heart to invest in other pastors. His church regularly invites groups of leaders from around the country to come and share ideas at Healing Place. You'll find Dino talking on his phone or drinking coffee at Starbucks with local pastors weekly. Dino's life exemplifies the principle that ministry friendship builds bridges for kingdom wins.

To reach out to other pastors, Dino has a few suggestions (all of which he practices):

- Get to know pastors' birthdays and anniversaries, along with important church dates (like building openings). Send a note with a gift.
- Take up an offering to help other churches with their building programs.
- Send a card and a gift to every new pastor in town.

When I had Dino and other pastors over to my house for dinner, he showed up with a note for my wife and a two hundred dollar Target gift card.

When I asked about his motivation for helping other churches, Dino said that when he started the church, he felt very alone. When he received a check from John Osteen (Joel Osteen's dad), Dino was deeply moved. "I guess that started a ball rolling for us that really just developed into who we are."

Dino and his church are passing along this blessing by contributing 10 percent of their annual missions budget to the Association of Related Churches, a group that has planted forty-four churches in the past four years.

Dino believes it is virtually impossible to be a biblical church leader and not be kingdom-minded. He says, "I think the way to encourage someone to see the value of relationships in the work of the kingdom is to demonstrate it to them, so that's why we give to, serve, and reach out to pastors of all kinds. Plus, I really feel like that is what Christ wants to do in the world." Dino is well known for saying, "It is amazing what gets accomplished when no one cares who gets the credit. We have to lay down the egos and the logos and just go get it done for Jesus."

Dino stresses the truth that followers of Christ are on the same team. He sets the example and encourages others to do their part to tear down the walls that separate us and to connect heart to heart instead of comparing style with style or going head to head with other churches. Dino says, "There are two different types of people: church builders or kingdom builders. We believe we are not the only ones doing good … that thought of being the only one doing it right or doing it at all can lead to an arrogance that will isolate you. We value the 'all above me, myself, and I' approach. There is so much more freedom in operating like that."

PART THREE

WHAT IT MEANS TO GET it BACK AND GUARD it

When it comes to cooking, one dish I seldom mess up is boiling water. The ingredients are simple, cheap, and readily accessible. I can usually tell when the dish is done. (Bubbles. Watch for the bubbles.)

My extensive experience with this culinary specialty has provided me with a spiritual insight: getting and guarding *it* is a lot like boiling water.

First, both take heat of a sort. Boiling water takes physical heat, while *it* takes the heat of spiritual passion, as we've discussed in the earlier chapters of this book.

Second, as soon as you remove the heat, water stops boiling, and *it* disappears.

Third, to get back to either one, you have to repeat step 1: do what you did the first time ... apply heat.

And fourth, once you've got the water boiling and the *it* flowing, if you want to keep *it*, you have to keep on applying heat. In fact, to maintain *it*, you need to invite an expert Cook to apply heat into your life. And this is one time you shouldn't get out of the kitchen.

For these final two chapters, the most important chapters of this book, I invite you to my new show: *Cooking* It *with Craig.*

Don't sit back. Don't relax. Don't just watch me.

Get ready to take action. Get ready to get *hot!*

ELEVEN

DO YOU HAVE it?

DOES   **HAVE YOU?**

Learn as though you would never be able to master it; hold it as though you would be in fear of losing it.

—*Confucius*

One of the qualities of liberty is that, as long as it is being striven after, it goes on expanding. Therefore, the man who stands in the midst of the struggle and says, "I have it," merely shows by doing so that he has just lost it.

—*Henrik Ibsen*

We've come a long way together on our journey. We've seen how *it*-full ministries have a God-inspired vision and are focused on the things that really matter. We've embraced the truth that with-*it* people share *it* in a deep and sincere camaraderie. Our ministry innovation has increased with our increasing passion to share the gospel. We've acknowledged that we won't succeed perfectly at everything we do, and that failing is often a step toward succeeding.

And we're excited that as God gives us hearts that are focused out-ward and kingdom-minded, he tends to give us more of *it*.

Now let's dive into the most important material we'll cover in this book. If you want your ministry to have *it*, more impor-tant than anything else we've discussed, *you* must have *it*. When *it* has filtered through your heart — the rare combination of pas-sion, integrity, focus, faith, expectation, drive, hunger, and God's anointing — God tends to infuse your ministry with *it*. He blesses your work. People are changed. Leaders grow. Resources flow. The ministry seems to take on a life of its own. At times it seems like you're just hanging on for your life.

Have you noticed that new believers often have *it*? They're "unreasonably" excited about Christ. They think God is always speaking to them (and maybe he is). They see everything as spiritual (and they're probably right). They believe Jesus might return soon (which he very well could). Everything they do is focused on him.

They have *it*.

Then some more "mature" believer decides to help them to grow up. "This is just a phase you're going through," the mature believer explains. "It'll wear off." The seasoned person might describe how Moses once experienced God's presence and glowed. But the glow faded. And the longtime passionless Christian inad-vertently talks the new passionate believer into surrendering *it* and becoming like the rest of the dull Christians you and I both know (and sometimes are).

Something similar occasionally happens to ministers. Well-intentioned believers gladly surrender their lives to full-time vocational ministry. They dream of devoting the balance of their days to glorifying God and serving his people. Over time, though, the purity of our motives can become clouded. Without realizing it, we might position ourselves for promotion, posture ourselves to be noticed, or play church politics. We turn pro. What was once beautiful quickly turns ugly.

How I Lost *It*

I'm going to be honest with you. This part of my story is painful to tell. I pray it helps you. When I came to Christ, I had *it*. I knew God was with me. I knew God was speaking to me. I knew God was guiding me. And God blessed whatever I touched.

At the age of twenty-three, as a brand-new pastor, I had far more passion than wisdom. Like many wonderfully young and naive pastors, I didn't know what couldn't be done. So if I believed God led me to do something, even if everyone else disagreed, I followed what I understood to be God's voice.

At the time, I was acutely aware of what I didn't know. Without a seminary degree, I felt only slightly better than biblically illiterate. With limited leadership experience, I relied more on prayer than on knowledge. Without great leadership skills, I simply tried to treat people with love. Without tons of resources, I trusted God to use what little we had.

As a young pastor, with little thought about my future, I was simply trying to follow Jesus. Then one day someone told me that I might actually become a good pastor. I'd thought of God as a good God, but not of myself as a good minister. Those words rattled me, scared me, haunted me. Could I really become a good pastor? Maybe so. But if I could beome a good pastor, then that meant the opposite was also a possibility. I could also become a bad pastor.

How could I ever become good enough? And if I became good enough, could I stay good enough? What if I was good one day and not good the next? Suddenly I was emotionally thrust back to the time I spent in sales. My boss told me I was only as good as my last sale. I was beginning to feel the same way in ministry. I was only as good as my last sermon. Or the last meeting. Or the last membership class. I felt a pressure that I'd never known before.

Without even realizing it, I took my focus off the power of God and put it on my own performance. Almost instantly, I didn't have as much time to feed on God's Word. Instead I had

DO YOU HAVE it? DOES it HAVE YOU?

163

to produce challenging and entertaining sermons. Sermon preparation became a cheap substitute for real time in God's Word. Instead of praying passionately and consistently, as I had in the past, my longest prayers were usually the ones I prayed in public. Instead of developing friendships with people who didn't know Christ, I worked hard to appear spiritual in front of those who already did.

For years, I had *it*. Unknowingly, I abandoned *it* and tried to produce my version of *it* in my own strength.

It didn't work.

Shifting from *It*

No one would have noticed outwardly what started to happen inwardly. My focus had shifted — ever so slightly. I wasn't consumed by bad things; it's just that I wasn't consumed by the best things. I was more concerned about issues that had never crossed my mind before. I became obsessed with numbers, all sorts of numbers. Instead of measuring success by my obedience to God, I measured success by how many people showed up and how many guests returned.

I was also driven by appearances. With all my heart, I wanted to be that good pastor. Since people offered more verbal feedback than God did, they became my primary audience. I wanted them to know how hard I worked, how much I cared, and how devoted I was.

It's difficult to describe, but while doing the work of God, I drifted from God. So many of us do. As pastors, we wholeheartedly believe that God exists, but we often do ministry as if he doesn't. Our sermons are filled with faith, but our actions prove that we're devoid of it. Our public prayers declare that all things

WHAT IT MEANS TO GET it BACK AND GUARD it

are possible with God, but our leadership style says all things are possible if our efforts are good enough.

John the Baptist said in John 3:30 (NKJV), "[Jesus] must increase, but I must decrease." In ministry, sometimes we try to increase by our own efforts, not realizing that we're dialing down the influence of Christ. You could say that as we increase, *it* decreases.

Looking for *It* in All the Wrong Places

In the early years of our church, even though we had very few resources, we had God's presence and blessing. That's all we really needed. We had *it* in our hearts. And that passion for him mixed with his Spirit won people to Christ. As our church grew, so did our resources. Remember, *it* is not a result of resources (buildings, signs, mailings, lights, videos), but *it* does attract resources. Suddenly we could buy things that earlier were barely even a dream.

We could buy children's curriculum. We could start a mother's day out. We could print four-color bulletins. We could buy each staff member a computer. We could afford a video projector. (We could find a volunteer with all ten fingers to run it.) We could buy stage lights that didn't explode. If we didn't have something, we could just purchase it.

Don't miss the subtlety of what happened. When we had limited resources, God was our source. He was all we needed. Then when we had access to those things that were once far off, they slowly, and wrongly, became the answers to our problems.

Without realizing it, our team started to think, *If we don't have* it, *we can work for* it, *buy* it, *or create* it. In the meantime, we started to forget about the one that *it* was all about.

At the start, God was *it*. He was everything we needed. Now, we thought we needed certain things to grow. To us, it wasn't as much about God. It was about everything else. And we started to lose *it*. Why? Because when you start to trust outward and physical resources instead of the inward and spiritual truth, you'll always lose *it*.

What happened? It was as if our *it* tank sprang a slow, small leak. Over time, *it* wasn't as special as *it* was before. Not as many

people came to Christ. Fewer gave sacrificially. The number of people willing to serve decreased. We could sense we were losing *it*, so we decided we had to get *it* back.

In our minds that meant more creativity, more hard work, more ministries to draw people. We were wrong. We had slipped into the dangerous belief that we could create *it*. Or re-create *it*. In a very subtle (but sick) way, it stopped being about God and became about us.

Looking back, it seems so obvious. Before, when we had *it*, we had vision alignment and divine focus. Now with all the resources, we had the option to do new things. Just because we could didn't mean we should, but that didn't stop us. We tackled the new projects right and left while slowly walking away from what made *it* special in the first place.

In the early years we had an unmistakable camaraderie. We were a team. But as we wrongly believed we needed *things* to produce *it*, we started to compete for resources. Instead of completing each other, we started competing with each other. Team members became more self-centered, territorial, and dangerously competitive.

Earlier, with nothing much to lose, we regularly took big risks. Year after year, we'd bet the farm. Now that we had something to lose, we became more cautious, guarding what we already had. Instead of saying, "What do we have to lose? Let's go for it!" we found ourselves saying, "With so much at stake, we'd better play it safe." Instead of living by faith, we lived by logic.

It's amazing how ugly an *it*-less ministry can become. Whereas we were once generous and kingdom-minded, we started to have an unhealthy preoccupation with any church doing well. *What's their secret? How can we compete? Why is God blessing them more than he is blessing us?* Slowly but surely we were killing *it*.

One of the bigger blows to *it* was hiring new staff and recruiting volunteers without communicating what *it* was all about. We assumed they would understand the heart of *it*. In the old days, everyone did. But as new members joined the team, they mis-

WHAT IT MEANS TO GET **it** BACK AND GUARD **it**

interpreted *it*. Many simply didn't get *it*. What made the ministry special before were the unseen qualities in the hearts of the people. The new staff members didn't know the story, so they thought what made *it* special was what they could see with their eyes: the lights, the videos, the fancy kids' rooms. To have *it*, they assumed, we needed more bells and whistles. But what we really needed was more of what we had left behind: raw passion for God and for people.

Do You Have *It*?

The Righteous Brothers used to sing about losing "that lovin' feeling." Are you singing a similar lament right now? Do you need to humbly admit, "I've lost *it*"? If you once had *it*, and now you don't, you can identify with the Righteous Brothers. Losing *it* is always painful. Joe Maddon, the manager of the Tampa Bay Devil Rays, said, "When you have a big lead and are losing it, when that starts to occur, everything turns to slow time."[37]

You wouldn't be the first to lose ground. You can see people "lose it" in virtually every segment of society. One country can be a world power for decades or centuries before quietly fading. Companies rise and fall. Ministries climb and crash. Stocks soar and dip. A sports team may dominate one year and be at the bottom of the pack the next. Actors and actresses are "in" one month and "out" the next. Same with politicians, pastors, plumbers, pediatricians, professors, painters, podcasters, and pig farmers. Just because you have *it*, you're not guaranteed to keep *it*.

Do you have *it*?

Be honest. Do you have that something special that is from God and for God? Do you think more about pleasing him than strategizing how to grow your church? Do you desire his pleasure more than the applause of men? Are you more concerned with his opinion of you than with the opinions of people?

Hopefully you can confidently answer those questions with God-pleasing responses. If so, you probably have *it*.

For years I couldn't. I wanted to be noticed, appreciated, affirmed. I needed people to think well of me, speak highly of me, admire my leadership success. Sure I wanted to see people get saved and grow spiritually, but if I was honest, that wasn't what was driving me. Instead, I was haunted by the desire to prove myself to some unknown something or someone. If I did more, accomplished more, reached more, then maybe I'd be good enough.

If that's you today, you might do what I did. Cry. Repent. Plead with God, *Give* it *back! Give* it *back to me in a way that I'll never lose* it *again.*

Getting *It* Back

What do you do if you realize you've lost *it*? How do you get *it* back?

If I could put *it* in a bottle and give some of *it* to everyone, I'd do it in a second. But God is the one who gives *it*. And he seems to give *it* to those who want *it* — or more precisely, to those who want him and his will. Maybe it's time for you to ask him for *it*. For him to become the true center of your life.

I'll share with you my journey with God and how I got *it* back. Hopefully my story will spark the desire to again pursue God with your whole heart.

How did I get *it* back? First, I had to admit that I had lost *it*. That was hard for me. It probably won't be easy for you. By nature, most ministry leaders want to believe that we're right and that we're succeeding. Admitting to failure — especially spiritual failure — is tough. (My failure was precisely a spiritual one.) You might need to start with the confession, "I've lost *it*. I've taken my eyes off the prize. I've been distracted from a wholehearted pursuit of Christ."

You might have gotten slightly, or much more than slightly, off track. Or maybe this has happened to one of your colleagues or someone you mentor. Or even a buddy from seminary days. Maybe you allowed some sin into your life. Maybe you neglected some basic spiritual disciplines. Maybe you read your own positive press and started believing it. Or maybe you got sick of the criticism and just got ticked off. Maybe you gave and gave and gave and forgot how to receive from others. Maybe someone hurt you and you walled up. Maybe you offered your best, and it didn't feel like your best was good enough. Maybe you simply got tired and let down your guard. Whatever the situation, if you had *it* and lost *it*, admit it. That's what I did.

Second, decide to get *it* back. You have to want *it*. Joe Ballard said, "It makes you more hungry after losing it last year."[38] If you've lost *it*, maybe you'll now be hungrier for *it* than ever before. But let me be honest: some small adjustment isn't likely to bring *it* back. If all you needed was to tweak something, you'd have done that long ago. I'm guessing it'll take a significant change of direction or priorities. If you think you've found a quick fix, I guarantee it's not an *it*-fix.

In my case, I had to force myself to do something I considered pretty radical. I was so caught up in the "ministry world" that I was neglecting my relationship with God. It's safe to say I was obsessed with ministry. I read church magazines. I listened to pastors' sermons. I watched certain Christian broadcasts. I read my favorite pastors' books. I attended the best church conferences. I did these things and more — all the time.

Church consumed me. Church was first. God was second.

Okay, it was worse than that. God was fourth or fifth.

My role as a pastor was interfering with my passion for God, which ricocheted back and crippled my role as a pastor. And it was time to finally do something about it. Since I couldn't quit the ministry to redevelop my love for God, I simply quit devouring the distracting ministry information. I felt God wanted me to tear down my ministry idols. This was right for me. It's unlikely the same approach would be the right thing for you. But you might find this idea sparking another equally weird but divinely necessary one in your heart.

For two years, I fasted from ministry information. No more ministry books. No more ministry magazines. No more church conferences. No more listening to other pastors' sermons. Extreme ... I know. Instead, I read the Bible. And I prayed. And I fasted. And I read the Bible some more. Slowly, I started to fall in love with God again — not with his bride, the church. (She already has a husband, and it's not me.) He was doing something special in my heart that increased with intensity by the day. It was like I was becoming born again ... again. By that, I'm not making a theological statement; I'm just describing my perception of the experience.

DO YOU HAVE it? DOES it HAVE YOU?

169

I didn't lose my salvation only to regain it. I had lost that loving feeling but found *it* again in a new and meaningful way that I pray I'll never lose again.

The apostle Paul started a well-known church in Ephesus. In many ways, this church had *it*. Years later, John, who helped oversee this church after Paul, recorded a message from Jesus to the Ephesian church in Revelation 2:4 – 5. Jesus said, "Yet I hold this against you: You have forsaken your first love. Remember the height from which you have fallen! Repent and do the things you did at first."

Have you forsaken your first love? Be honest. Do you love ministry more than you love Christ? Do you care more about what people think about you than what God thinks about you? Do you strategize about ways to grow your ministry more than you think about how to grow God's people? Do you study the Bible to preach more often than you study it to hear from God? Do you pray more often in public than you do in private? Have you lost your first love?

Jesus said to remember the height from which you've fallen. Can you think back to a time when the only thing that mattered was doing what God wanted you to do? Do you remember craving his Word? Do you remember being excited about sharing your faith with anyone who would listen? Think back on what you had with God, that something special which is now gone.

Jesus said, "Repent," or in other words, "Turn around." Stop doing what you've been doing. Do what you used to do. If you used to pray, pray. If you used to fast, fast. If you used to love freely, love freely. If you once gave until you had little left and then you gave some more, give that way again. If you used to worship while driving, without caring who saw you, start worshiping again. If you used to have intimate spiritual friendships but got too busy, make time to rekindle those relationships or to start new ones. If you used to serve people with no strings attached, start serving again.

Several months ago I had lunch with a local pastor and friend. With deep emotion, he explained to me how he'd "lost it." One of his board members left the church and took several people with him. His church was behind budget. He didn't want to preach. He

WHAT IT MEANS TO GET it BACK AND GUARD it

didn't want to visit anyone in the hospital. He didn't want to read God's Word. He didn't even want to pray. After unloading plenty of hurt, my friend confided in me that if he weren't the pastor of his church, he wouldn't worship there.

I listened quietly, asking God for wisdom. I recognized his pain, understood his frustration, and related to his spiritual burnout. Knowing he needed my prayers more than my limited advice, I simply asked him if we could pray. Without much enthusiasm, he agreed to let me pray. So I simply asked God to "disturb him" in a big way.

Nothing significant happened that day.

A couple of months later, my friend called and shouted, "I'm disturbed! I'm disturbed!" He explained with great joy how God had disturbed him. My friend had suddenly become disgusted with his sin of spiritual complacency. He was disturbed by the lukewarmness in his church. He was disturbed by those in need. He was disturbed by people who were without Christ.

As he opened God's Word, his hunger for God increased. Deciding to fast, he denied his body nutrition, seeking only to be filled by God. With time, his love for people grew, his passion to preach increased, he fell in love with Jesus again — all by doing the things he did at first. God disturbed him, in the best sort of way.

If you've lost *it*, God knows where *it* is. You can find *it* by doing the things that once brought *it* to you. Your relationship with God is only as good as you want it to be.

What are you waiting for? Seek him.

Now.

IT FACTORS

- If you want your ministry to have *it*, more important than anything else we've discussed, *you* must have *it*.
- As we increase, *it* decreases.
- If you think you can buy *it*, you've already lost *it*.
- You might need to start with the confession, "I've lost *it*. I've taken my eyes off the prize. I've been distracted from a wholehearted pursuit of Christ."
- Ask God to give *it* back.
- To get *it* back, do the things that brought *it* before.

it FACTORS

WHAT IT MEANS TO GET it BACK AND GUARD it

Questions for Discussion or Reflection

1 Name someone or some organization that had *it* and lost *it*. What happened? Why did they lose *it*? What do you think it would take for them to get *it* back?

2 Do you have *it*? If so, what is contributing to *it*? If your answer is no, when did you start to lose *it*? What changed in you? How have you taken your eyes off of Christ?

3 How well are you communicating the heart of *it* to those who are new to your ministry? Do new attenders get *it*? What about volunteers? How about staff members? If they don't understand what God is doing, how can you better express *it*?

4 If you've lost *it*, it will probably take more than some small adjustment to recover *it*. What radical step could you take to get *it* back (or to get more of *it*)? What about the leaders of your church? Is there something you used to do that contributed to *it* that you no longer do? What is God calling you to do that you have been neglecting?

DO YOU HAVE it? DOES it HAVE YOU?

173

TWELVE

GUARDING it

HOW TO KEEP it ONCE YOU HAVE it

I consider my life worth nothing to me, if only I may finish the race and complete the task the Lord Jesus has given me — the task of testifying to the gospel of God's grace.

—the apostle Paul (Acts 20:24)

i am sitting at my computer with tears forming. I am praying, but not with words. This prayer is born in my heart. At this very moment, I'm aware of God's presence. He is here, with me. I'm sitting in a comfortable chair, typing these words and over-whelmed by God. As I'm typing — or trying to — I am worshiping him, needing him, crying to him. Nothing is wrong. My family is healthy. Our church is growing. Life is good. Yet everything is wrong. As good as everything appears, I'm in spiritual agony. I hurt for people, deeply. I cry often. I wake up at night and pray for hours before falling back to sleep. I'm consumed with the burdens of God. Others see our church and say it is succeeding. I feel like we're failing.

We're so big. We've done so little.

It's not that I'm depressed. It's quite the opposite. The fire of God's presence is burning within me, consuming me. When I say

"consuming me," that's exactly what I mean. It is burning away the worst parts of me. I can relate to the words of Paul: "I have been crucified with Christ and I no longer live, but Christ lives in me. The life I live in the body, I live by faith in the Son of God, who loved me and gave himself for me" (Gal. 2:20).

I have *it* — again.

And I never want to lose *it*.

If you don't have *it*, I pray you'll get *it* back. Once you get *it* — the passion, the fire, the purity, the hunger for God — I pray you'll keep *it* always. I know what it's like to have *it* and lose *it*.

I want to always walk closely with God, enjoying his consistent presence and direction. So I've made three prayers a part of my daily prayer life. These heartfelt and dangerous prayers have helped me to keep *it*.

Stretch Me

When you become comfortable in your relationship with God, you'll lose *it*. (By comfortable, I mean complacent, lazy, and distracted.) In many ways, comfort is an enemy of faith. Hebrews 11:6 says, "And without faith it is impossible to please God." Jesus pleaded with his followers, knowing the time was short, reminding them always to "be on guard! Be alert!" (Mark 13:33). That's why we'll constantly want to ask God to stretch us.

Recently, while swimming with my kids, I met another dad who was a coach. After some casual conversation, he asked me in a competitive dad-to-dad sort of way, "How long do you think you can hold your breath underwater?" Even at the age of forty, I could feel the rush of excitement anticipating a contest between men. *He doesn't know who he's talking to*, I thought smugly. *I grew up watching Aquaman!*

WHAT IT MEANS TO GET it BACK AND GUARD it

"I don't know," I replied, my heart pumping. "Maybe a minute." This was quite a humble response; I secretly believed I could do more than that.

He challenged me to give it a try, and seconds later I was underwater ready to prove my aquamanhood.

As the seconds slowly ticked by, I felt my lungs tighten. Panic set in. *Could I drown doing this?* Deciding that drowning is better than losing, I stayed under. I could feel my face turn blue. My eyes opened wider. *Longer. Longer. Just a few seconds longer.* Finally, after what seemed like a lifetime, I burst out of the water gasping for air. *I was still alive!*

The coach smiled and said, "Impressive! You stayed under for one minute and twelve seconds!"

That's what I'm talkin' *about.*

The coach said, "What would you say if I told you that I could help you double your time?" *What?* I'd been played. He wasn't going to compete against me. *The wimp!* He was trying to teach me some sort of "I'm a coach and you're not" lesson. Maybe he didn't know that I almost died moments ago.

"You're smokin' weed," I blurted. "That's what I'd say."

The coach continued, his tone more fatherly. "If you pay attention, I'll teach you something that will inspire you to do even more than you've ever done before."

He had my full attention.

The coach began to talk to me almost hypnotically, explaining a calming technique that was sure to increase my time. "You can do much more than you realize," he assured me. "Your body can survive underwater for several minutes. Your mind doesn't believe that. Your greatest limitation is your mind. You must silence your mind. Take four deep breaths. Slide slowly into the water. Close your eyes. Remain perfectly still. When your lungs tighten, don't worry. You still have a lot more time. When you think you can't go on, open your eyes. Focus on something. Count slowly to twenty. When you get to twenty, count again."

Armed with this advice, I followed his instructions. After four breaths, I calmly slid underwater. I tried my best to turn off my mind. When my lungs tightened, I relaxed. When I hit my limit, I opened my eyes and counted. Then I counted some more. Every few seconds, my coach said, "More ... you have more in you. More ... you have more in you."

Finally I had enough and came up for air. This time when I came out of the water, my coach was beaming as he told me that my new record was 2:45. Do you understand those numbers? (And that little two-dot thingy in the middle?) Two minutes and forty-five seconds!

I was elated, pumped, jazzed, and shocked. *How did I do that? I stayed underwater for almost three whole minutes.* I didn't know I had that in me.

Then the coach looked me in the eye and said, "You have more in you than you realize. God has put more in you than anyone knows."

God spoke to me that day. About more than oxygenation potential. That's why I now regularly say to him, *Stretch me.*

I'd like to say the coach's words to you. *You have more in you than you realize. God has put more in you than anyone knows.*

Ask him to stretch you. Then let him.

God wants to stretch you. He wants you to live by faith, to believe him. It will mean putting yourself in new environments. Experiencing something new. Something different.

Ask God to stretch you. Then follow his direction. He might direct you to change your leadership style or the way you preach. He might challenge you to go to a third-world country and leave behind part of your heart. He might ask you to give like you've never given before. He might lead you to do something your closest friends believe is foolish and impossible. He might introduce you to a new church leader who will rock your comfortable world. Or maybe to a lost person who is far from God.

WHAT IT MEANS TO GET it BACK AND GUARD it

Let him stretch you. Attempt what others say can't be done. You have more in you than you realize. God has put more in you than anyone else sees.

Ask God to stretch you. As he does, you might start to find *it* again.

Ruin Me

On Sunday, October 8, 1871, Dwight L. Moody was finishing his Sunday evening sermon when the city fire bell began to ring. Realizing that much of the city was burning, Moody's first concern was for his family. Rushing to a close, he asked the people to evaluate their standing with God and return the next week. Little did he know, many of them would never return. They would die in the worst fire in Chicago's history.

Later, Moody agonized, wondering if any of the deceased died without Christ. They were in his church building and he let them leave without confronting their own sin. Broken and changed, Moody vowed to God he'd never hold back again. Every time he stood before a crowd, he would plead with them to follow Christ. D. L. Moody was ruined — in a very good way.

Whenever I meet someone who has *it* — a heart abandoned for Christ — I'm meeting ruined people. I'm not talking about a destructive ruin. Sin destroys and ruins. Burnout can destroy and ruin. Anger can destroy and ruin. I'm referring to the work of a loving God who breaks us and ruins us for his glory. Josh Billings said, "Life is short, but it's long enough to ruin any man who wants to be ruined."[39] Maybe it's time to let God ruin you.

Let me explain. I have a friend named Mark Button. Mark has *it*. He was the co-founder of Koosh Toys, developers of the koosh ball and the vortex football. (And I invented the technique that allows me to throw a vortex football farther than you ever could. Seriously, I'm ready when you are. Bring it on.) (My koosh ball skills are not so impressive, but give me time ...)

For several years, Mark and his wife, Ronnie, tried to get pregnant, only to be disappointed month after month. After years of shattered expectations, Mark and Ronnie discovered they were pregnant. Not with one child, not with two, but with triplets! God had answered their prayers. Times three.

Or so they thought.

The pregnancy proceeded perfectly until Mother's Day. That was the day Ronnie was admitted to the hospital with an excruciating headache and died suddenly, along with her three babies, the victim of a brain aneurysm. I have to wipe tears away every time I think about Mark's loss. He had every physical thing a person could want, but lost the people he loved the most.

Ruined.

This tragedy happened over ten years ago. Since then, Mark has remarried and God has blessed his new family with healthy children. When I asked him what he's most excited about today, he looked at me sincerely and said, "God uses me to ruin people." Because of his business experience, Mark has many influential friends. His goal is to take some of the greatest leaders in the country to one of the poorest corners of the world — and ruin them.

Mark exposes people to things they prefer to ignore and lets God wreck them. Do you want *it*? Ask God to ruin you in a good way. Let him break your heart. Allow him to give you what my friend Bill Hybels calls "holy discontent." Let God crush you with a burden.

As I look back on my life, when I had *it*, I was ruined. God had messed me up for his purposes. All I thought about was him. Pleasing him. Obeying him. Talking about him. When I saw people without Christ, my heart ached deeply for them. Sharing Christ consumed me. I wasn't good for much else. I was ruined.

Over time, though, I slipped back into normal routines. I didn't care as much about people. I didn't care as much about God. I wasn't ruined anymore, and I didn't have *it*.

Like Isaiah, I was of more use to God when I was ruined. You might relate to an episode in Isaiah's story recorded in Isaiah 6. It was the year King Uzziah died. Which is a polite way of saying, "This was the year when the world as we knew it ended." And in the worst time Isaiah could imagine, he saw the Lord. And he got *it*. Verse 5 records his thoughts when he experienced the pure presence of God: "Woe to me!" he cried. "I am *ruined*! For I am a man of unclean lips, and I live among a people of unclean lips, and my eyes have seen the King, the LORD Almighty" (emphasis mine).

Isaiah would never be the same. He had experienced God. The experience squashed him flat, squeezed out all his pride, emptied him of self-ambition. Now he was suitable for God's purpose, for the greatest fulfillment Isaiah could ever find. With *it*, Isaiah was now fully available to God. When God asked who he should send with a message to his people, Isaiah blurted, "Here am I. Send me!" (v. 8).

As I reflect on the seasons of my life when I lived without *it*, I remember God trying to ruin me. But I fought it off. In ministry, I had built a wall of protection around my heart. Honestly, I thought this was a strength, something necessary to survive.

Whenever I'd visit with someone who was hurting, I'd separate my feelings from the conversation, thinking this would help me be a better pastor. When someone faced a tragedy, like an accidental death or a suicide, I managed to stay strong, never showing weakness.

Maybe you've fallen prey to the same fallacy. You might think, *But if I allow myself to break down, I'll be a wreck for my family. I won't be able to survive emotionally. The people who trust me will stop consulting me.* Yes, those are legitimate concerns, but you might be surprised at the results of dropping your emotional shields. Your family might be overjoyed to share with you in your hurts. God might sustain you emotionally and spiritually in ways that have never crossed your mind. And those who look to you could be inspired by your vulnerability. Sure it will feel risky. But it's more risky to stay walled up.

Over the years, God exposed me time and again to things that could've ruined me in a good way. On April 19, 1995, Timothy McVeigh detonated a bomb across the street from the church I served in Oklahoma City. That bomb killed 181 people. The shock waves echoed across the globe as CNN showed pictures of the carnage. For me it was more than images flickering on the TV. The rescue workers used our church lobby as a morgue. When I walked by and saw the mangled bodies of men, women, and little children, my stomach turned, but I didn't let it ruin me.

That wasn't the only time I responded to deep need so dispassionately. When my mentor and close friend fell into sin and later took his life, I was left stunned, speechless, and emotionally devastated. I sensed God was trying to use this tragedy to break open my heart with love again. Resisting God's wise, good hammer and chisel, I quickly pulled myself up by my bootstraps, fighting to be strong for others, and didn't let even this ruin me as I should have.

When I visited the poor in a third-world country and held the tiny fragile hands of children who hadn't eaten for days, it bothered me, confused me, shook me. Seeing these innocent children suffering aroused a mix of emotions — rage, depression, and everything in between. Although this experience could have ruined me in a good way, I somehow managed to stuff the emotions and get back to life as normal.

God tried to ruin me. I didn't let *it* happen.

Three years ago, my wife's brother, David, died at the age of thirty-four. To say this impacted a lot of lives would be the understatement of this book. Seeing our family let him go somehow startled me back to my neglected spiritual reality. His funeral was one of the more sobering moments of our lives. Life is short. Eternity is real. And I wasn't doing much about it.

That's when I started to evaluate my leadership at the church. From an outsider's perspective, we were wildly successful. But were we? Were we really? Would it really matter in our communities if our church wasn't there? Was God pleased? Was I being obedient as a leader?

Finally, I surrendered to his plan. With a repentant and soft heart, I wanted *it* back — the zeal for him, the desire to please him, the passion for people. So I said from the bottom of my heart, *Okay, God, you want to ruin me, go ahead. Do it. Ruin me through and through.*

And he did.

WHAT IT MEANS TO GET it BACK AND GUARD it

Now, instead of being rock solid in my emotions, I cry often. I tear up when people hurt. I carry their burdens home with me. I care deeply about people who are in need. Suffering bothers me. Injustice haunts me. When I know someone who is hurting, it wrecks me.

If you want to keep *it*, and I know you do, ask God to ruin you. Expose yourself to something that you know will move you. Don't shrink back. Don't fight your emotions. Don't lay another brick atop your self-made wall of protection. Give in to the heart. Feed the hurt. Let *it* grow. Let *it* bother you. Invite *it* to overtake you.

God loves to give *it* to ruined people.

Heal Me

I pray God is stretching you. And I pray that he will ruin you. My third prayer is that he will heal you. And he will, if you sincerely ask him to. You might think, *But I'm not sick*. Maybe not physically, but if you're like most people I know, you have some wounds that God wants to heal.

Those who have *it*, and keep *it*, are those who are healing and growing. One of my spiritual heroes is in his eighties. Every time we talk he tells me about some new insight God is showing him. Last time we visited, he said, "I didn't realize I was so full of pride." Then he explained how God is cleansing his heart of pride. Hearing an eighty-something-year-old express how God continues to heal him inspires me.

To be healed, we have to first admit to the ways we're sick or in need. You might have to face something you've stuffed, ignored, or rationalized for years. Are you ready to confess your need? To make it easier on you, I'll go first.

I'm an addict.

No, I don't have a sexual addiction. I'm not addicted to alcohol, illegal drugs, prescription medicine, or the lottery. And I'm not going to deliver a clever punch line, like, "Actually, I have three addictions — to the Father, Son, and Holy Spirit!" or, "I'm addicted to studying the Bible." I have a serious addiction that I'm working hard to overcome. Thankfully, with a lot of prayer and hard work, I'm making significant progress.

Truth is, many of us are addicted. Some addictions are frowned upon. Others often go unmentioned. Some are even readily accepted. You might have one of the "acceptable" addictions. For example:

Some are addicted to pleasing people.

Some are addicted to perfection.

Some are addicted to email or blogging.

Some are addicted to work.

Me? I'm addicted to adrenaline. You could say I'm an adrenaline junkie.

You might think, *Well, that's no big deal.* Actually, it *is* a big deal. It's dangerous. And I'm fighting to overcome it. My body craves the adrenaline rush. Usually adrenaline is our good friend. God gave our bodies adrenaline to handle challenging situations. But for some of us, our bodies crave the rush of that performance-enhancing hormone.

Here is how it affects me: If there are no leadership emergencies, I subconsciously crave some problem to solve. I desire action. When things are slow, I panic and create things to do. I have a very hard time relaxing. When I do relax, it's by taking a hard bike ride, lifting weights, playing tennis, or reading a book related to work, ministry, or leadership.

In other words, I don't often relax.

Way too many times, I'm with my family, but I'm not all there. As my mind is consumed with church-related thoughts, my kids are bouncing off the walls trying to get my attention. I'll never forget when my third daughter, with tears in her eyes, asked, "Why don't you listen to me when I'm talking? Do you even love me?" Sobering words. While my family begs for my attention, my mind is generally racing, working, strategizing. When I do finally relax, generally after about four days off, my body starts to "thaw out." I can feel my heart rate and breathing slow. My face tingles. Once I finally settle down, I become the nice, laid-back Craig — until I go back to work and the dangerous cycle repeats itself.

WHAT IT MEANS TO GET it BACK AND GUARD it

Can you relate? Maybe it's not an addiction to adrenaline, but you might have an equally dangerous and vulnerable need. To be honest, I've been talking with a counselor for help. For years, I thought seeking professional help was a sign of weakness. I couldn't have been more wrong. Together, with the help of my wife, my counselor, and my close friends, I've been making significant progress.

Will you be honest with yourself for a moment? Do you have a hard time trusting? Have you been burned by church members and find it difficult to have friends? Are you distant from your spouse? Do people tell you that you're a control freak? Do you find yourself on a high when people brag on you and a low when they criticize you? Do you feel good about yourself when your ministry is growing and depressed when it is not? Do you have a secret sin? Or a fantasy life? Are you overly critical and jealous? Do you feel like you never quite measure up?

I've shared with you three prayers that are an important part of my life. I'm wondering, should they have a place in your life?

Stretch me.

Ruin me.

Heal me.

May God Bless You

Thank you for hanging in here with me through this whole book. We've traveled a long way together. It has been an honor to share with you. Parts of the book may have been painful to read. Parts were certainly painful for me to write. Hopefully God is stirring you, drawing you, speaking to you. When he does, I know you'll follow his lead.

Before wrapping up, I'd like to encourage you to meet with the leaders of your ministry. Discuss the questions at the end of each chapter. You might have *it*, but those you're with might not. I believe God wants to use you to help them get *it*.

Once you do get *it*, never take *it* for granted. Embrace the power of the Holy Spirit working in you to do more than you can ask or imagine. To help you get *it* and keep *it*, I'll share part of a Franciscan benediction. This is my final prayer for you:

May God bless you with discomfort at easy answers, half truths, and superficial relationships, so that you may live deep within your heart.

May God bless you with anger at injustice, oppression, and the exploitation of people, so that you may work for justice, freedom, and peace.

May God bless you with tears to shed for those who suffer from pain, rejection, and starvation, so that you may reach out your hand to comfort them and to turn their pain into joy.

And may God bless you with enough foolishness to believe that you can make a difference in this world, so that you can do what others claim cannot be done.

That's *it*. Amen.

- You have more in you than you realize. God has put more in you than anyone knows. Ask him to stretch you. And let him.
- If you want to keep *it*, and I know you do, ask God to ruin you. Expose yourself to something that you know will move you. Feed the hurt. Let *it* grow. Let *it* bother you. Invite *it* to overtake you.

it FACTORS

Questions for Discussion or Reflection

1 How is your church leadership allowing God to stretch you? What do you need to expose yourself to in order to break out of a slump? Is God leading you to attempt something that you've not yet attempted? What are you going to do about it?

2 What is God using to ruin you in a good way? Is there something that bothers you that you've been avoiding?

3 Do you have an addiction you need to address? Does a part of your heart need healing? Have you been hurt or disillusioned and need God's healing? What do you think God wants to do about it?

4 Reread the Franciscan benediction. What is God saying to you through that prayer? What is God saying to the leaders of your ministry?

NOTES

1. Sam Chand, *Ladder Focus* (Highland Park, IL: Mall Publishing, 2007), 24 – 25.
2. Ibid., 21.
3. *www.helium.com/tm/395126/anthony-robbins-reason-achieve.*
4. Thom Rainer and Eric Geiger, *Simple Church* (Nashville: B & H Publishing Group, 2006), 76.
5. *www.usatoday.com/money/workplace/2007-08-01-work-friends_N.htm.*
6. *www.changeboard.com/hrcircles/blogs/hrarticles/archive/2007/08/23/getting-engaged-on-the-job-do-you-have-a-best-friend-at-work-the-gallup-organization.aspx.*
7. *www.barna.org/FlexPage.aspx?Page=Topic&TopicID=34.*
8. *www.cybernation.com/quotationcenter/quoteshow.php?id=6817.*
9. *thinkexist.com/quotation/the_way_a_team_plays_as_a_whole_determines_its/154041.html.*
10. *www.wow4u.com/mother-teresa/index.html.*
11. *wilderdom.com/teambuilding/Quotes.html.*
12. *www.associatedcontent.com/article/91148/transparency_in_relationships.html.*
13. *thinkexist.com/quotation/the_more_you_praise_and_celebrate_your_life-the/217679.html.*
14. *www.basketball-plays-and-tips.com/basketball-motivative-quotes.html.*
15. *www.maximumimpact.com/newsletters/leadership/archives/2007/10_8.txt.*
16. *cms.skidmore.edu/ctm/quotes.cfm.*
17. *www.innovationtools.com/Quotes/QuotesDetail.asp?CatID=17.*
18. *www.innovationtools.com/Quotes/Quotes.asp.*
19. *thinkexist.com/quotes/roger_enrico/.*
20. *www.incwell.com/Biographies/Edison.html.*
21. *www.leadershipnow.com/creativityquotes.html.*
22. *thinkexist.com/quotation/when-you-innovate-you-ve-got-to-be-prepared-for/384348.html.*
23. *www.bible.org/illus.php?topic_id=823.*
24. *www.lib.fit.edu/pubs/librarydisplays/InventionsMar04.htm.*

25. Tom Kelley, *The Ten Faces of Innovation* (New York: Currency, 2005), 2.
26. *creativequotations.com/one/352.htm.*
27. *www.youtube.com/watch?v=fsZghCZlkxY.* (From a Nike commercial.)
28. Seth Godin, *Small Is the New Big* (New York: Penguin, 2006), 124.
29. *creatingminds.org/quotes/failure.htm.*
30. *thinkexist.com/search/searchquotation.asp?search=we+seem+to+ gain&q=author%3A%22Leo+F.+Buscaglia%22.*
31. *www.brainyquote.com/quotes/authors/s/samuel_beckett.html.*
32. *thinkexist.com/quotation/courage_is_going_from_failure_to_ failure_without/150101.html.*
33. *www.sermonillustrations.com/a-z/w/witnessing.htm.*
34. *www.pietyhilldesign.com/gcq/quotepages/unity.html.*
35. *jmm.aaa.net.au/articles/4477.htm.*
36. *www.coolquotes.com/quotes/alan_redpath.html.*
37. *thinkexist.com/services/bookmark.asp?id=726790&quote=when- you-have-a-big-lead-and-are-losing-it-when.*
38. *thinkexist.com/quotes/Joe_Ballard/.*
39. *www.brainyquote.com/quotes/authors/j/josh_billings.html.*

Craig Groeschel is the founding and senior pastor of LifeChurch.tv. Craig, his wife, Amy, and their six children live in the Edmond, Oklahoma, area, where LifeChurch.tv began in 1996.

Craig's creative leadership skills are changing the way church is done worldwide. Under his leadership, LifeChurch.tv has become one of the country's first multicampus churches, with over fifty weekend worship experiences at thirteen different locations throughout the United States.

Craig and Bobby Gruenewald write daily blog posts for pastors. You can participate in this blogging community at swerve.lifechurch.tv.

Craig Groeschel and LifeChurch.tv not only have it, they know what it's like to have it, lose it, and get it back again. Craig pulls back the curtain and offers lessons and insights that will help any spiritual leader better fulfill God's vision and calling.

—*Larry Osborne, author and pastor, North Coast Church*

Craig Groeschel and the LifeCurch.tv team are serial innovators whose passionate commitment to introducing what's new, making it work, and giving it away are powerfully impacting the church today.

—*Greg Ligon, vice president and publisher, Leadership Network*

Craig Groeschel is one of the most visionary yet down-to-earth leaders I know. If you're looking for a book that will help take your church to the next level, this is it.

—*Mark Batterson, lead pastor, National Community Church*

Respecting this mystery of how God works, Craig masterfully guides you to peek behind the veil to understand what energizes the breathtaking movement of God we all deeply desire.

—*John Burke, author of* No Perfect People Allowed

This book is not just theoretical but is one of the most practical ministry books I have read in years.

—*Dan Kimball, author of* They Like Jesus but Not the Church

It

How Churches and Leaders Can Get It and Keep It

Craig Groeschel

Craig Groeschel, founding and senior pastor of LifeChurch.tv, takes
you on a nine-session video journey
to discover the powerful presence from God that he calls
IT at work in many churches. Each video session is approximately ten minutes long and focuses on the questions: "What
is IT, and where did IT come from?"

Craig will explore the necessary contributions to IT such
as vision, divine focus, unmistakable camaraderie, innovative
minds, willingness to fall short, hearts focused outward and
kingdom-mindedness. He concludes the video experience
with a session on "Do you have IT? And how to keep IT once
you have IT."

This video is designed for leadership groups and church
groups and includes discussion questions on the DVD at the
end of each session.

DVD: 978-0-310-94213-9